HOLY YEAR
2000
the Great Jubilee

VATICANVS

LOZZI **R**oma

edizioni turistiche

Direzione e redazione:

LOZZI ROMA sas
Via Filippo Nicolai, 91 - 00136 ROMA
Tel. 06 35497051 - Tel. e Fax 06 35497074
e-mail: lozzirm@spinweb.it

Stampato presso la tipografia
Arti Grafiche F. Garroni
Via Prospero Santacroce, 47
00100 Roma

Fotolito: TIPOCROM srl - Roma

Referenze fotografiche:

Le immagini dei mosaici dei Pontefici da pagina 28 a 35 sono state gentilmente concesse dalla Basilica di San Paolo fuori le Mura - Roma.
Archivio fotografico dell'Osservatore Romano.
Archivio fotografico della Reverenda Fabbrica di San Pietro.
Archivio fotografico LOZZI ROMA s.a.s.

On the following page: The Holy Year 1900. Pope Leo XIII opens the Holy Door at St. Peter's.

INDEX

The calendar of the Holy Year 2000

DECEMBER 1999

24 Friday. Solemnity of the Birth of the Lord. *St. Peter's Basilica.* **Opening of the Holy Door. Mass at Midnight.**

25 Saturday. Solemnity of the Birth of the Lord. *Basilicas of St. John Lateran and Santa Maria Maggiore.* **Opening of the Holy Door.** Mass during the Day. *St. Peter's Basilica.* **"Urbi et Orbi" Blessing.**

31 Friday. *St. Peter's Basilica.* **Prayer vigil for the passage to the Year 2000.**

JANUARY 2000

1 Saturday. Solemnity of Mary, Mother of God. *St. Peter's Basilica.* **World Day of Peace.**

2 Sunday. *St. Peter's Basilica.*
Day for Children.

6 Thursday. Solemnity of the Epiphany of the Lord. *St. Peter's Basilica.* Holy Mass. Episcopal Ordinations.

9 Sunday. Feast of the Baptism of the Lord. Holy Mass. **Celebration of the sacrament of Baptism for children.**

18 Tuesday. Beginning of the Week of Prayer for Christian Unity. *Basilica of St. Paul-Outside-the-Walls.* **Opening of the Holy Door.**

25 Tuesday. Feast of the Conversion of St. Paul. *Basilica of St. Paul-Outside-the-Walls.* Ecumenical celebration for the conclusion of the Week of Prayer for Christian Unity.

28 Friday. Memorial of St. Ephrem. *Basilica of St. Cecilia in Trastevere.* Divine Liturgy in the East Syrian Rite (Chaldean and Malabarese).

FEBRUARY 2000

2 Wednesday. Feast of the Presentation of the Lord. *St. Peter's Basilica.* Liturgy of light and Holy Mass. **Jubilee of Consecrated Life.**

9 Wednesday. Memorial of St. Maron. *Basilica of Santa Maria Maggiore.* Divine Liturgy in the **Syro-Antiochene Rite** (Maronite).

11 Friday. Memorial of Our Lady of Lourdes. *St. Peter's Basilica.* Holy Mass. Celebration of the Sacrament of the Anointing of the Sick. **Jubilee of the sick and health-care workers.**

18 Friday. Memorial of Blessed John (Beato Angelico). *Santa Maria "sopra Minerva".* **Jubilee of artists.**

20 Sunday. Jubilee of permanent deacons.

22 Tuesday. Solemnity of the Chair of St. Peter Apostle. *St. Peter's Basilica.* Holy Mass. **Jubilee of the Roman Curia.**

MARCH 2000

5 Sunday. *St. Peter's Basilica.* **Beatification-Canonization.**

8 Wednesday. Ash Wednesday. Penitential procession from the *Basilica of St. Sabina to the Circus Maximus.* Holy Mass and imposition of ashes. Request for pardon.

12 Sunday. First Sunday of Lent. *Basilica of St. John Lateran.* Rite of Election and the enrolment of the names of the catechumens.

19 Sunday. Second Sunday of Lent. *Basilica of St. John Lateran.* First scrutiny of catechumens.

20 Monday. Solemnity of St. Joseph. **Jubilee of craftsmen.**

25 Saturday. Solemnity of the Annunciation of the Lord. Nazareth Basilica of the Annunciation. Liturgical celebration linked with the *Basilica of Santa Maria Maggiore.*

26 Sunday. Third Sunday of Lent. *Basilica of St. John Lateran.* Second scrutiny of catechumens.

APRIL 2000

2 Sunday. Fourth Sunday of Lent. *Basilica of St. John Lateran.* Third scrutiny of catechumens.

9 Sunday. Fifth Sunday of Lent. *Basilica of St. John Lateran.* Rite of giving the Creed and the Lord's Prayer to the catechumens.

10 Monday. Jubilee of migrants and refugees.

16 Sunday. Palm Sunday of the Lord's Passion. *St. Peter's Square.* Commemoration of the Lord's entry into Jerusalem and Holy Mass.
18 Tuesday. Tuesday of Holy Week. *Major Basilicas.* Communal celebration of the sacrament of Penance with individual absolution.
20 Thursday. Holy Thursday. *St. Peter's Basilica.* Chrism Mass. *Basilica of St. John Lateran.* Mass of the Lord's Supper.
21 Friday. Good Friday. *St. Peter's Basilica.* **Celebration of the Lord's Passion. Colosseum, Solemn Way of the Cross.**
23 Sunday. Easter Sunday. *St. Peter's Basilica.* **Easter Vigil of the Holy Night:** Service of Light, Liturgy of the Word, Baptismal Liturgy (Celebration of the Rite of Christian Initiation of Adults), Eucharistic Liturgy.
St. Peter's Basilica. Mass during the Day. **"Urbi et Orbi" Blessing.**

MAY 2000

1 Monday. Memorial of St. Joseph the Worker. Holy Mass. **Jubilee of workers.**
7 Sunday. Third Sunday of Easter. *Colosseum.* **Ecumenical service for the "new martyrs".**
14 Sunday. Fourth Sunday of Easter. *St. Peter's Basilica.* Holy Mass. Priestly Ordinations. **World Day of Prayer for Vocations.**
18 Thursday. 80th Birthday of the Holy Father. *St. Peter's Square.* **Jubilee of clergy.**
25 Thursday. Jubilee of scientists.
26 Friday. *Basilica of St. Mary of the Angels.* Divine Liturgy in the Alexandrian-Ethiopian Rite.
28 Sunday. Sixth Sunday of Easter. Holy Mass. **Jubilee of the Diocese of Rome.**
31 Wednesday. Vigil of the Solemnity of the Ascension of the Lord. *St. Peter's Basilica.* **First Vespers of the Solemnity.**

JULY 2000

2 Sunday. Station Mass of the Jubilee.
9 Sunday. Jubilee celebration in the prisons.
16 Sunday. Station Mass of the Jubilee.
23 Sunday. Station Mass of the Jubilee.
30 Sunday. Station Mass of the Jubilee.

AUGUST 2000

5 Saturday. Vigil of the Feast of the Transfiguration of the Lord. *Basilica of St. Mary Major.* **Prayer vigil.**
6 Sunday. Feast of the Transfiguration of the Lord. *Basilica of St. Paul-Outside-the-Walls.* **Second Vespers of the Feast.**
14 Monday. Vigil of the Solemnity of the Assumption of the Blessed Virgin Mary. *Basilica of Santa Maria Maggiore.* Incense Rite of the Coptic Liturgy.
15 Tuesday. Solemnity of the Assumption of the Blessed Virgin Mary. **Opening of the 15th World Youth Day.**
19 Saturday – 20 Sunday. Prayer Vigil and Holy Mass. **Conclusion of the 15th World Youth Day. Jubilee of youth.**
27 Sunday. Station Mass of the Jubilee.

SEPTEMBER 2000

3 Sunday. *St. Peter's Basilica.* **Beatification-Canonization.**
8 Friday. Feast of the Birth of the Blessed Virgin Mary. **Solemn Celebration to recall the birth of the Mother of the Lord.**
10 Sunday. *St. Peter's Basilica.* Holy Mass. **Jubilee of university teachers.**
14 Thursday. Feast of the Exaltation of the Holy Cross. From the *Basilica of the Holy Cross in Jerusalem* to the *Basilica of St. John Lateran.* Vespers in the Armenian Rite and the Rite of Antasdan.
15 Friday. Opening of the International Marian-Mariological Congress.
17 Sunday. Jubilee of senior citizens
24 Sunday. Holy Mass. **Conclusion of the International Marian-Mariological Congress.**

OCTOBER 2000

1 Sunday. Feast of the Pokrov (Protection of the Mother of God). *Basilica of St. Maria "sopra Minerva".* Divine Liturgy and the Akathistos Hymn in the Byzantine Rite.
3 Tuesday. Day for Jewish – Christian Dialogue.
7 Saturday. Memorial of Our Lady of the Rosary. **Recitation of the Rosary and torchlight procession.**

8 Sunday. *St. Peter's Basilica.* Holy Mass. **Jubilee of Bishops on the occasion of the 10th Ordinary General Assembly of the Synod of Bishops.** Act of dedicating the new millennium to the protection of Mary.

14 Saturday – 15 Sunday. Third Worldwide Meeting of the Holy Father with Families.

15 Sunday. *St. Peter's Square.* Holy Mass. Celebration of the Sacrament of Matrimony. **Jubilee of families.**

20 Friday – 22 Sunday. International Missionary-Missiological Congress.

22 Sunday. *St. Peter's Basilica.* Holy Mass. **World Mission Day.**

29 Sunday. *Olympic Stadium.* Holy Mass. **Jubilee of athletes.**

31 Tuesday. Vigil of the Solemnity of All Saints. *St. Peter's Basilica.* First Vespers of the Solemnity.

NOVEMBER 2000

1 Wednesday. Solemnity of All Saints. *St. Peter's Basilica.* **Beatification/Canonization.**

2 Thursday. Commemoration of All the Faithful Departed.

5 Sunday. Holy Mass. **Jubilee of those involved in public life.**

12 Sunday. Holy Mass. Day of thanks for the gifts of creation. **Jubilee of the agricultural world.**

19 Sunday. *St. Peter's Basilica.* Holy Mass. **Jubilee of the military and the police.**

21 Tuesday. Feast of the Presentation of the Blessed Virgin Mary.

24 Friday. Opening of the World Congress for the Apostolate of the Laity.

26 Sunday. Solemnity of Christ the King. *St. Peter's Basilica.* Conclusion of the World Congress for the Apostolate of the Laity.

DECEMBER 2000

2 Saturday. Vigil of the First Sunday of Advent. *St. Peter's Basilica.* First Vespers of Sunday.

3 Sunday. First Sunday of Advent. *Basilica of St. Paul-Outside-the-Walls.* Holy Mass.

8 Friday. Solemnity of the Immaculate Conception of the Blessed Virgin Mary. *Basilica of Santa Maria Maggiore.* Akathistos Hymn.

10 Sunday. Second Sunday of Advent. *Basilica of St. John Lateran.* Holy Mass.

17 Sunday. Third Sunday of Advent. *Basilica of St. Paul-Outside-the-Walls.* Holy Mass. **Jubilee of the entertainment world.**

24 Sunday Solemnity of the Birth of Our Lord. *St. Peter's Basilica.* **Midnight Mass.**

25 Monday. Solemnity of the Birth of Our Lord. *St. Peter's Basilica.* Mass during the Day. **"Urbi et Orbi" Blessing.**

31 Sunday. St. Peter's Basilica. Prayer Vigil for the passage to the new millennium.

JANUARY 2001

1 Monday. Solemnity of Mary Mother of God. *St. Peter's Basilica.* Holy Mass. **World Day of Peace**

5 Thursday. Vigil of the Solemnity of the Epiphany of the Lord. *Basilicas of St. John Lateran, St. Mary Major and St. Paul-Outside-the-Walls.* Holy Mass. **Closing of the Holy Door.**

6 Friday. Solemnity of the Epiphany of the Lord. *St. Peter's Basilica.* **Closing of the Holy Door.**

The Holy Year of 1983. Pope John Paul II kneeling before crossing the threshold of the Holy Door.

The religious significance and the history of the Jubilee

In the Catholic tradition, the Jubilee year is a great religious event. It is the year of the remission of sins and the punishment for sins; it is the year of reconciliation among enemies, of the conversion and the penitence of the sacrament.

The Jubilee is commonly called the "Holy Year" not only because it begins, progresses and concludes with solemn sacred rites, but also because it is destined to promote the sanctity of life. In fact, it was instituted to consolidate the faith, favor the works of solidarity and the fraternal communion inside the Church and in society, and to recall and stimulate the believers toward a more sincere and coherent profession of faith in Christ, the only Savior. During the Holy Year, the faithful can acquire the **Jubilee indulgence** that coincides with the remission before God of the temporal punishment for already-pardoned sins, which the Church concedes to individual Christians through the fulfilment of certain deeds determined by the pontifical authority. From the theological point of view, the Jubilee is defined as a "solemn plenary indulgence conceded by the Roman pontificate with special faculty for the confessors in favor of the faithful."

The Jubilee Year traces its origins to the Old Testament. The law of Moses determined that there would be a special year every fifty years for the Jewish people: *"You will declare holy the fiftieth year and you will proclaim the liberation of the country for all of its inhabitants. Everyone will go back to his own property and family. The fiftieth year will be jubilant; you will not sow nor harvest, as the fields will produce by themselves, nor gather the grapes to make wine from the un-pruned vines. Since it is the Jubilee, you will hold it sacred; you may, however, eat the products of the earth. In this year of the Jubilee, everyone returns to possess his own"* (Book of Leviticus). The celebrations were announced by the sound of a ram's horn, which in Hebrew is called "Jobhel", from which the word Jubilee is derived. The celebration of this year brought, among other things, the restitution of the earth to the ancient proprietors, the remission of debts, the liberation of slaves and the fallow of the land.

In the New Testament, Jesus presents himself as He who fulfils the ancient Jubilee, having come to *"preach the year of the grace of God"* (Isaiah). The Jubilee therefore expresses joy, because the Christian community is full of joy for the rescue that springs from penitence, from confession, from communion and from prayer.

Rome will be the place in which, according to the intentions of the Pontificate of the Church, the *"Coming Third Millenium"* will be celebrated.

"Aperite mihi portas iustitiae", with these words on Christmas Eve before the Jubilee Year, the pope knocks three times with a silver hammer at the holy door, walled up since the end of the previous Holy Year. Then the penitentiary cardinal knocks, and when the wall which covers the door is removed, some penitentiaries wash the threshold of the Holy Door. Then the pope will cross the doorway carrying a candle in his left hand and a cross in his right hand. This ritual will be repeated in the other Patriarchal Basilicas in Rome (San Giovanni in Laterano, Santa Maria Maggiore and San Paolo Fuori Le Mura) where the arch-priests will open the respective Holy Doors.

The Jubilee Year is either ordinary, when tied to a regular schedule, or extraordinary, when it has been declared for some event of particular importance. There have been twenty-five regular Jubilees celebrated; the Holy Year 2000 will be the twenty-sixth. The tradition of declaring a Jubilee dates to the 16th century; their duration varied from a few days to a year. The last extraordinary Holy Years of this century were declared in 1933 by Pope Pius XI for the 19th centennial of the Redemption, and in 1983, by John Paul II to celebrate 1950 years since the Redemption. In 1987, Pope John Paul II also declared a year in honor of the Virgin Mary.

The Holy Year 2000 assumes a special importance because it will celebrate the 2000-year anniversary of the birth of Christ. In addition, it will be the first Holy Year that falls between the end of one millenium and the beginning of another: the first Jubilee Year, in fact, was declared by Pope Boniface VIII in 1300. The Jubilee of the year 2000 will serve as a great prayer of praise and gratitude for the gift of the Incarnation and Redemption of the Son of God. The same John Paul II has explained the reason for the new Holy Year in the apostolic letter *"Tertio Millennio Adveniente"*: "the two thousand years since the birth of Christ represent an extraordinary Jubilee, not only for Christians, but indirectly for all of humanity".

St. Peter's Square, with the 16th century fountain, designed by Carlo Fontana, in the foreground.

The Jubilee Years through the centuries

It is the first of January **1300**: crowds of pilgrims come from the farthest countries of Europe to kneel down on the Tomb of St. Peter. They ask Pope Boniface VIII to concede particular spiritual benefits, especially considering that the Jubilee Year has a particular meaning. It is a spontaneous popular request, which probably originated from various penitentiary movements in the Christian world during the previous century. It is enough to recall the shining figure of St. Francis of Assisi, who symbolises such movements, in order to understand its nature and its significance. This popular origin is confirmed by a peculiar episode reported by an indisputable witness, Cardinal Stefaneschi: a 107 year-old man coming from the Savoia Province started his trip toward Rome, recalling that a hundred years before, when he was

only seven, he had done the same pilgrimage with his father. He had promised his father that, if he were still alive, he would have continued the tradition of his ancestors by repeating the same pilgrimage one hundred years later; according to this story, "anyone who visits the bodies of the Apostles on the centenary, dies free of guilt and pain". Other French pilgrims, among them two very old men from Beauvais, agreed on the truth of this story. These witnesses have strongly influenced popular opinion.

The Holy Pontiff granted the request that same year. On February 22 (a holiday for St. Peter's Basilica), with the Seal *Antiquorum Habet Fida Relatio*, he proclaimed the first Jubilee Year in the history of Christianity. Although he firmly asserted papal supremacy - even in the political field -

Pope Boniface VIII inaugurates the first Holy Year in 1300, in a fresco by Giotto.

John Paul II.

Boniface VIII certainly would have never thought that seven centuries later, countless streams of pilgrims coming from the farthest reaches of the world would have repeated with great devotion the ritual visit to the Basilicas, in order to follow a tradition that has changed very little over the centuries. The Bull, in fact, granted a Plenary Indulgence to all those who in 1300 and in every centennial year since visited the Basilicas of St. Peter and St. Paul "with reverence and really repented and confessed".

This historic declaration was much talked about throughout the Christian world; a large number of pilgrims crowded the roads to the Eternal City, and in particular those that led to the Vatican Basilica. According to the clear description in Dante's Inferno (Canto XVIII, lines 28-32), on that occasion the Sant'Angelo Bridge, which leads to St. Peter's basilica, was divided in two by a fence in order to control the traffic flow.

The celebration of the Jubilee Year in 1300 was the last great Roman event before the Avignonese exile of the Church: in 1305, in fact, the Holy See had to move to Avignon, in Provence, where for more than seventy years the Pope bore the humiliating role of "Chaplain of the King of France". After having given hospitality to a countless number of pilgrims, Rome became depopulated, almost like a village, and fell prey to the discord among rival families. Nevertheless, the ideal of its ancient greatness was still alive: Cola di Rienzo, a genial plebian figure, tried to restore its classical splendor, but he held power for only a brief, tumultuous period. Nevertheless, the Eternal City remained the vibrant centre of Christianity. In fact, in 1343 Clement VI was asked to proclaim from Avignon the Second Jubilee Year, to be celebrated in Rome in 1350, even though, as we have seen, Pope Boniface VIII had originally determined that the Holy Years be separated by one hundred years. Clement VI not only confirmed the unique role of Rome as guardian of the Apostles' Tombs, he included the venerable Cathedral of Rome, St. John Lateran, among the basilicas worthy of being visited.

The third Jubilee Year was celebrated in 1390, as if to ratify the recent return of the Popes from their exile in Avignon to the real Roman See; a move opposed by the French Cardinals. Pope Boniface IX decreed the periodicity of the Holy Years to be 33 years, in memory of the length of the Jesus' life on earth; he also granted the enlargement of the Jubilee privilege, after the end of the Roman Jubilee Year, to other cities. This innovation was obviously accepted with great enthusiasm by those who found it impossible to

The hammer and trower, in gilded silver and ivory, given to Pope Pius XI for the Holy Year 1925.

reach Rome. In this way, the celebrations lasted almost a decade, to reach the "Centenary". Then, as happened a century before, countless streams of pilgrims arrived in Rome, and Boniface IX willingly granted the request of proclaiming the fourth Jubilee Year in 1400, at a distance of only ten years from the previous one.

On the occasion of the Jubilee Year of 1423, which was announced to coincide with the end of the Western Schism that had deeply lacerated and divided Christianity, Pope Martin V found the city in such poor condition (after more than a century of abandonment) that it did not even look like a city.

Although marred by the black death and by a terrible disaster (two hundred people pushed by the crowd, because of the restiveness of some horses, fell from Saint Angel Bridge and from the bank of the Tiber, drowning miserably in the river), the Jubilee Year of 1450 had a great resonance in the artistic and cultural world.

The Jubilee Year was announced by Nicholas V, a "Humanist" Pope who confronted the difficult task of reconciling the Christian religion with the celebration and revival of classical Greek and Roman culture; it was celebrated in a city reborn to new life, and served - along with Florence, Venice and Naples - as one of the great cultural centres of the peninsula.

With the Seal *Ineffabilis Providentia* of April 17, 1470, Paul II reduced the normal interval be-

Above, Castel Sant'Angelo.

To the right, an antique print representing pilgrims crossing Ponte Sant'Angelo toward St. Peter's during the Jubilee celebrations of the 18th century.

The Pantheon (I-II century). It was transformed from a pagan temple to a Christian church in 609 by Pope Boniface IV, who dedicated it to the Madonna and the Martyrs. During the Holy Year 1400, the church was added to the other Jubilee sites.

mony that still symbolises quite visibly the beginning of the Jubilee Year took place for the first time: the opening of the screen of the Holy Door of St. Peter's.

Twenty-five years afterwards (**1525**), at the opening of the ninth Jubilee Year, dark clouds appeared over the church and Italy: In 1517 Martin Luther started the Protestant Reformation, after which extreme disagreements took place not only in the strictly religious field, but also in the political and military fields. The wars that befell Europe in the first half of the XVI century were fought on religious pretence, in order to hide the aggression that pit one state against the other. As usual, it was the people who suffered through the decade-long incursions of the opposing armies. Just two years after the celebration of the Jubilee Year 1525, even Rome was invaded: the Lansquenets, the notorious soldiers of Charles V (who also fought

tween Jubilee Years to twenty-five years. Sistus IV proclaimed a new Jubilee Year (**1475**), and prepared the city by settling the roads and repairing the most important Basilicas. By then the Renaissance spirit was in full force, decay of the preceding century had been brought the a halt, a tireless campaign of urban renewal had begun, destined to restore Rome to its majesty and splendour.

For the Jubilee Year of **1500**, the third centenary Jubilee, Alexander VI Borgia (who was considered an unreliable Pope for many reasons) introduced a custom still in force: he opened the Holy Doors in the main Basilicas during the entire Jubilee Year, not only for practical reasons (namely to encourage the introduction of the believers), but also "in order to symbolize the easiest entry to the divine mercy by gaining the Jubilee Indulgence", according to the words of Paul VI. On Christmas Night, 1499, the cere-

The Quirinal Palace was built in the Holy Year 1575 as the summer residence for the pope. Today it is the seat of the President of the Italian Republic.

Above. Piazza Navona. It was the site of a phantasmagoric procession staged to celebrate the Holy Year 1650. Immense altars were set up at either end of the piazza, dedicated to the Resurrection of Christ and the Assumption of Mary to Heaven. Fireworks were set off in the center of the piazza, right next to the Fountain of the Four Rivers, which had been built by Bernini to commemorate that same Holy Year.

To the left. Campo de' Fiori. The Dominican monk Giordano Bruno was condemned for heresy during the Inquisition and burned at the stake here during the Holy Year 1600. His statue stands at the center of the piazza.

The Trevi Fountain. The tradition of tossing a coin in this fountain to ensure a return to Rome takes on an even greater significance during the Holy Year.

against the German Protestant princes) subjected the city to one of the most cruel and devastating sacks in its history.

This disadvantageous situation might have led to the cancellation of the Jubilee of 1525. But the Pontificate did not want to renounce it, and accepting in part the issues which had generated the Lutheran protest, it prohibited the request for money in exchange for Jubilee indulgences. Meanwhile, to promote the religious character of the Holy Year, new celebrations of the mysteries of the Passion

Play took place in the Colosseum. As the site carried symbolic significance for the martyrdom of Christians there, it became the seat of the celebration of the Passion of Christ and the Martyrs.

By the middle of the century, the storm had finally passed: in **1550**, Julius III wanted to celebrate both the Jubilee Year and his accession to the throne of St. Peter on February 8th. The Pope took severe measures that demonstrated his desire to prevent the Jubilee pilgrimage from ending in tragedy for the visitors, as had happened in the

The Spanish Steps on Piazza di Spagna, built for Pope Benedict XIII by the architect De Sanctis for the Holy Year 1725.

past. He imposed a price controls on necessary goods, rent control and a tax for the restoration and the care of the roads and a tax against the tradesmen, who took great advantage of the endless stream of pilgrims.

The atmosphere in which the eleventh Jubilee Year was proclaimed in 1575 was altogether different. The treaty of Cateau-Cambrésis, signed in 1559, had ended (at least for that century) the great European wars, while in 1563 the Council of Trent had concluded with the signing of the fundamental points of the Catholic Reform (also known as Counter-Reformation). The Jubilee proclaimed by Gregory XIII was characterised by a severe abolition, as suggested by the famous Cardinal Borromeo, of any "earthly" characteristic that might corrupt the religious atmosphere. Masks and games were therefore prohibited, while acts of devotion and humbleness emphasised the penitential character of the event. In this Holy Year the number of Jubilee churches grew to seven, with the addition of the Churches of San Sebastiano, San Lorenzo fuori le Mura and Santa Croce in Gerusalemme.

The Colosseum. In the cavea of the Amphitheatre, St. Leonard presented the Stations of the Cross for the first time during the Holy Year 1475.

The arrival of the 17th century brought one of the most memorable **Jubilee Years in 1600**. In an atmosphere of "austerity" inaugurated by the preceding Jubilee Year, the abolition of masks and carnival processions (that were particularly appreciated in Rome until the previous century) was confirmed. This century did not, however, lack for displays of particular splendour and ostentation, particularly the splendid ride of the Spanish Viceroy of Naples, Don Ferrante di Castro, who arrived in Rome at the head of a cavalcade of eight hundred horses, luxuriously harnessed and mounted by riders dressed with sumptuous liveries. More than 1500 citizens, welcomed and served in great luxury at the banquet given by the Viceroy. The popular celebrations of that Jubilee Year were certainly more suitable to a genuine penitential atmosphere: for example, there was the Holy Representation with which, on May 9, the "Compagnia di Misericordia" (Company of Mercy) made its entry in Rome by walking through the Porta del Popolo and along the streets of the city by candlelight, representing the scenes of the Passion, the Death and the Resurrection of Christ.

It is worth noting the tragic circumstance of the **Jubilee Year of 1625**, which was marred by the plague that, in those times, was quite frequent and very difficult to avoid. Nevertheless, the flux of pilgrims did not falter, and Pope Urban VIII had to face major problems with public order caused by tussles over who got traffic precedence, particularly felt in that century characterised by proud obstinacies.

The embellishment of the city and the restoration of its monuments continued. In fact, the ancient venerable residence of the Popes next to the Basilica of St. John Lateran, in the care of the Cardinal Francesco Barberini, was the first to be restored.

The **Jubilee Year of 1700** is instead recalled mainly for the humility and charity that led to the election that year of Pope Innocent XII. After having begged the Cardinals gathered in Conclave to exempt him from the supreme mission because he did not feel spiritually prepared, he accepted their firm will. He went on to perform His highest mission with the same humility: his first visits were dedicated to the ill pilgrims who were taken in hostels made ready for them, stopping at their beds with an affability that had no precedent.

Among the other Jubilee Years of the 18th century, the one celebrated in **1750** by Benedict XIV, who had won great popularity while known as Cardinal Lambertini, distinctly emerges. Although the rational atmosphere of the 18th century was not too favourable, the eighteenth Jubilee Year had excellent results. While it is true that the splendid, luxurious processions characteristic of the 17th century were missing, this must not be considered a drawback, at least from the religious perspective. Instead, the best preachers gathered in Rome, spreading among the faithful citizens the spirit of sincere, deep devotion that characterised that pope. Already established as the theatre of the representation of the Mysteries of the Passion by 1525, in December 1750 the Colosseum was con-

Pope John Paul II celebrates the traditional Stations of the Cross on Good Friday at the Colosseum.

St. Peter's Square crowded with thousands of the faithful for a solemn celebration of the Holy Year.

secrated in the name of the passion of the Christian Martyrs by Pope Benedict XIV, who also initiated the celebration of the Stations of the Cross. This transformation into a sacred meeting place for the faithful brought an end to the decay of the Colosseum. The altars and the stations of the Via Crucis, built over the course of the 17th and 18th centuries, are no longer visible. (Nevertheless, the Pope still celebrates a moving night-time Stations of the Cross in front of an illuminated Colosseum during the Holy Week before Easter). Also on the occasion of the Holy Year 1750, the late-Baroque façade of the Basilica of Santa Maria Maggiore was completed by Ferdinando Fuga.

During the 19th century, the historic events which involved all of Europe caused more than an interruption in the rhythm which the Jubilee

Years had until then followed: the **Jubilee Year of 1800** could not be celebrated because of the disorder that the Napoleonic armies had caused at the end of the French Revolution, especially in Italy. In fact, Pius VI died in exile at Valence on August 29, 1799. His successor, Pius VII, elected on March 14, 1800, did not consider it right to announce the Jubilee Year because of the "upset conditions in Christianity".

Even in the middle of the century it was necessary to renounce the celebration of the Jubilee Year: the uprisings of 1848 had upset Europe, and reached Rome, where Pope Pius IX had to escape, taking shelter at Gaeta, during the proclamation of the Roman Republic. Pius IX, however, had the chance to celebrate the **Jubilee Year in 1875**, thanks to the exceptionally long period of

St. Peter's Basilica. The Holy Door (exterior).

stead, free of "the lead ball" of temporal power, according to the definition given by Paul VI, the Church could dedicate itself more strongly than in the preceding centuries to a more authentic ecumenism, which transcended territorial and political boundaries.

The **Jubilee Year of 1925**, twenty-third of the series, came after a tragic twenty-five year period. The First World War had ended only seven years before, and in much of Europe the liberal democracies, the protagonists of 19th century history, were in crisis, giving rise to dictatorial regimes that, as we all know, dragged Europe and the whole world toward a new and even bloodier war. This outcome, nevertheless, was quite distant and unforeseeable in 1925; the Jubilee Year remains memorable mostly for its modern mark that showed the capacity of the Church to adapt itself to the changing times, while keeping the most important religious values, traditions and customs.

A detailed and faithful witness to the events of the twenty-third Holy Year is furnished by the precious volume in which, for the first time, the Roman Curia wrote a complete report of the actions linked with the organization of the Jubilee

St. Peter's Basilica. The Holy Door (inside).

his Pontificate. This was the first one celebrated after the papacy lost its temporal power on September 20, 1870, after Rome had been captured on behalf of the "bersaglieri" of the Italian Army and proclaimed capital of the united Italy. The small territory of the Vatican City remained as a guarantee for papal independence. Paradoxically, it was at exactly that time that the Jubilee Year celebrations began again regularly, despite the terrible world wars and turmoil that have changed the world through the century.

At the beginning of the **20th century** (1900), the twenty-first Jubilee Year proclaimed by Pope Leo XIII reflected the new times. The openness toward the great masses, already ratified by the first social encyclical of the Church, the *Rerum Novarum*, edited by Leo XIII himself in 1893, has a great resonance; after a long period of stagnation related to the two proceeding centuries, the Jubilee Year saw thousands of pilgrims coming again to Rome by all means that progress had offered. The Jubilee Year also showed that the end of the secular power of the Church, realised with the capture of Rome in 1870, had not at all produced, as the extremists had darkly forecast, an enslavement of the Church to the Italian State. In-

John Paul II blesses the faithful gathered in St. Peter's Square.

Year. In this way, a new tradition began which put a series of documentary sources of great interest at the disposal of historians. In **1933**, an extraordinary Jubilee Year was proclaimed by Pius XI in order to worthily celebrate the 19th centennial of the Redemption of the human race that took place with the Death and the Resurrection of Jesus. Also in this case, the results of progress were put to use: for the first time, the Vatican Radio broadcast the voice coming from the smallest, but most potent State in the world.

The twenty-fourth Jubilee Year, solemnly celebrated in **1950**, marked the end of the second and even more terrible post-war period of our century in Italy. With its impressive participation, the Catholic world seemed to emphasise the end of the fears and nightmares and the return to peace. By every means possible, from bicycle to aeroplane, horse to the most modern ship, more than two and a half million pilgrims came from all over the world, crowding the streets of Rome. It is enough to make a meaningful comparison to recall that in 1925 Rome welcomed almost 600,000 pilgrims, and that during the twenty-fourth Jubilee Year, their number was more than quadrupled. The twenty-fourth Jubilee Year was characterised by the celebration of many beatifications and canonizations, and most of all by the proclamation of the Dogma of the Assumption before more than six hundred bishops surrounded by an endless stream of Christians.

The **Jubilee of 1975** was part of an ecclesiastical renewal that had begun with the Second Vatican Council, which had concluded ten years earlier. This Jubilee Year was totally in line with the Council, both for important and significant innovations of a liturgical nature (which have been discussed in the preceding chapter) and for the spirit of reconciliation with ourselves, our brothers, and God, which Pope Paul VI had indicated as a fundamental moment and essential character of the twenty-fifth Jubilee, the "Jubilee of Jubilees". On Christmas night in 1974, the inaugural ceremony of the Jubilee was followed contemporaneously by people all over the world for the first time in history, thanks to television.

The Holy Year 1975 concluded with an expectation that the Holy Door would have been re-opened at the end of the millennium. But with great surprise, Pope John Paul II proclaimed Easter **1983** as the beginning of an extraordinary Holy Year. It was called the *"Jubilee of the Redemption"*, a reference to the sacrifice of Jesus as an enormous opportunity for humanity to find its own redemption. This Holy Year took place 50 years after the extraordinary Jubilee of 1933, in which the 1900th anniversary of the death of Christ was celebrated. This was the first Holy Year in which Rome lost its centrality, as all of the dioceses in the world were given the possibility to introduce some local Jubilee churches. Those who came to Rome were not constrained to visit each of the four patriarchal basilicas; it was enough to visit one, or one of the Catacombs, or the Basilica of Santa Croce in Gerusalemme.

The **Great Jubilee of the Year 2000**, the twenty-sixth Holy Year in history, will open in the name of the joy and thanksgiving for the grace of God that manifested itself in the Incarnation of the Son of God. In fact, it will celebrate 2000th anniversary of the birth of Jesus, along with the beginning of the new millennium in Rome as well as in the Holy Land.

For the city of Rome, 2000 will be an exceptional year. An estimated 26 million pilgrims will converge upon the city, affirming once again its centrality to Christian civilisation, as a cosmopolitan city open to people from all around the world. The expectations for the year 2000, aside from those associated with the end of the millennium, come on the wake of the growing ecumenical role of the Church, significantly symbolised by the figure of Pope John Paul II, the first non-Italian pope elected in more than four centuries. He has dedicated his pontificate to the vibrant and untiring contact with all the people of the world.

Crowd in St. Peterís Square during a Holy Year celebration in 1875.

BULL OF INDICTION
OF THE GREAT JUBILEE OF THE YEAR 2000
by John Paul II

INCARNATIONIS MYSTERIUM

JOHN PAUL BISHOP SERVANT OF THE SERVANTS OF GOD
TO ALL THE FAITHFUL JOURNEYING TOWARDS THE THIRD MILLENNIUM
HEALTH AND THE APOSTOLIC BLESSING

1. Contemplating the mystery of the Incarnation of the Son of God, the Church prepares to cross the threshold of the Third Millennium. (...)

2.The Great Jubilee of the Year 2000 is almost upon us. Ever since my first Encyclical Letter Redemptor Hominis, I have looked towards this occasion with the sole purpose of preparing everyone to be docile to the working of the Spirit. The event will be celebrated simultaneously in Rome and in all the particular Churches around the world, and it will have, as it were, two centres: on the one hand, the City where Providence chose to place the See of the Successor of Peter, and on the other hand, the Holy Land, where the Son of God was born as man, taking our flesh from a Virgin whose name was Mary (cf. Lk 1:27). With equal dignity and significance, therefore, the Jubilee will be celebrated not only in Rome but also in the Land which is rightly called "Holy" because it was there that Jesus was born and died. (...)

5. How many historic memories the Jubilee evokes! We can recall the year 1300 when, responding to the wish of the people of Rome, Pope Boniface VIII solemnly inaugurated the first Jubilee in history. Resuming an ancient tradition which offered "abundant remission and pardon of sins" to those who visited Saint Peter's Basilica in the Eternal City, he wished on that occasion to grant "a pardon of sins which would be not only more abundant, but complete". From that time onwards, the Church has always celebrated Jubilees as significant steps on her journey towards the fulness of Christ. (...)

6. (...) I therefore decree that the Great Jubilee of the Year 2000 will begin on Christmas Eve 1999, with the opening of the holy door in Saint Peter's Basilica in the Vatican, a few hours before the inaugural celebration planned for Jerusalem and Bethlehem and the opening of the holy door in each of the other Patriarchal Basilicas of Rome. At Saint Paul's Basilica, the holy door will be opened on Tuesday, 18 January, when the Week of Prayer for Christian Unity begins, as a way of emphasizing the distinctive ecumenical character of this Jubilee.

I also decree that in the particular Churches the Jubilee will begin on the most holy day of the Nativity of the Lord Jesus, with a solemn Eucharistic Liturgy presided over by the diocesan Bishop in the Cathedral, as also in the Co-Cathedral where the Bishop may delegate someone else to preside at the celebration. Since the rite of the opening of the holy door is proper to the Vatican Basilica and the other Patriarchal Basilicas, it would be appropriate that the opening of the Jubilee in the individual Dioceses be done by having the statio in one church and a procession from there to the Cathedral, by liturgical reverencing of the Book

of the Gospels and a reading of parts of this Bull, in accordance with the directives of the "Ritual for the Celebration of the Great Jubilee in Particular Churches".

May Christmas 1999 be for everyone a feast filled with light, the prelude to an especially deep experience of grace and divine mercy, which will continue until the closing of the Jubilee Year on the day of the Epiphany of Our Lord Jesus Christ, 6 January 2001. (...)

7. (...) Pilgrimages have always been a significant part of the life of the faithful, assuming different cultural forms in different ages. A pilgrimage evokes the believer's personal journey in the footsteps of the Redeemer: it is an exercise of practical asceticism, of repentance for human weaknesses, of constant vigilance over one's own frailty, of interior preparation for a change of heart. Through vigils, fasting and prayer, the pilgrim progresses along the path of Christian perfection, striving to attain, with the support of God's grace, "the state of the perfect man, to the measure of the full maturity of Christ" (Eph 4:13). (...)

11. (...) As the Successor of Peter, I ask that in this year of mercy the Church, strong in the holiness which she receives from her Lord, should kneel before God and implore forgiveness for the past and present sins of her sons and daughters. (...)

Joannes Paulus PP. II

GIVEN IN ROME, AT SAINT PETER'S, ON 29 NOVEMBER, THE FIRST SUNDAY OF ADVENT, IN THE YEAR OF OUR LORD 1998, THE TWENTY-FIRST OF MY PONTIFICATE.

CONDITIONS FOR GAINING
THE JUBILEE INDULGENCE

By the present decree, which implements the will of the Holy Father expressed in the Bull of Indiction of the Great Jubilee of the Year 2000, and by virtue of faculties granted by the same Supreme Pontiff, the Apostolic Penitentiary defines the discipline to be observed for gaining the Jubilee indulgence.

All the faithful, properly prepared, can fully enjoy, throughout the Jubilee, the gift of the indulgence, (...) by satisfying the necessary conditions. The faithful can gain the *Jubilee indulgence:*

1) In Rome, if they make a pious pilgrimage to one of the Patriarchal Basilicas, namely, the Basilica of *Saint Peter in the Vatican*, the *Archbasilica of the Most Holy Saviour at the Lateran*, the *Basilica of Saint Mary Major* and the *Basilica of Saint Paul* on the Ostian Way, and there take part devoutly in Holy Mass or another liturgical celebration such as Lauds or Vespers, or some pious exercise (e.g., the Stations of the Cross, the Rosary, the recitation of the Akathistos Hymn in honour of the Mother of God); furthermore, if they visit, as a group or individually, one of the four Patriarchal Basilicas and there spend some time in Eucharistic adoration and pious mediations, ending with the "Our Father", the profession of faith in any approved form, and prayer to the Blessed Virgin Mary.

To the four Patriarchal Basilicas are added, on this special occasion of the Great Jubilee, the following further places, under the same conditions: the *Basilica of the Holy Cross in Jerusalem, the Basilica of Saint Lawrence in Campo Verano, the Shrine of Our Lady of Divine Love,* and the *Christian Catacombs.*

2) In the Holy Land, if, keeping the same conditions, they visit the *Basilica of the Holy Sepulchre in Jerusalem,* or the *Basilica of the Nativity in Bethlehem* or the *Basilica of the Annunciation in Nazareth.*

3) In other ecclesiastical territories, if they make a sacred pilgrimage to the Cathedral Church or to other Churches or places designated by the Ordinary, and there assist devoutly at a liturgical celebration or other pious exercise, such as those mentioned above for the City of Rome; in addition, if they visit, in a group or individually, the Cathedral Church or a Shrine designated by the Ordinary, and there spend some time in pious meditation, ending with the "Our Father", the profession of faith in any approved form, and prayer to the Blessed Virgin Mary.

4) In any place, if they visit for a suitable time their brothers and sisters in need or in difficulty (the sick, the imprisoned, the elderly living alone, the handicapped, etc.), as if making a pilgrimage to Christ present in them (cf. Mt 25:34-36), and fulfiling the usual spiritual and sacramental conditions and saying the usual prayers. The faithful will certainly wish to repeat these visits throughout the Holy Year, since on each occasion they can gain the plenary indulgence.

The plenary indulgence of the Jubilee can also be gained through actions which express in a practical and generous way the penitential spirit which is, as it were, the heart of the Jubilee. This would include abstaining for at least one whole day from unnecessary consumption (e.g., from smoking or alcohol, or fasting or practising abstinence according to the general rules of the Church and the norms laid down by the Bishops' Conferences) and donating a proportionate sum of money to the poor; supporting by a significant contribution works of a religious or social nature (especially for the benefit of abandoned children, young people in trouble, the elderly in need, foreigners in various countries seeking better living conditions); devoting a suitable portion of personal free time to activities benefiting the community, or other similar forms of personal sacrifice.

William Wakefield Card. Baum (Major Penitentiary)

Rome, at the Apostolic Penitentiary, on 29 November 1998, the First Sunday of Advent.

St. Peter's Basilica. The tomb of Pope Clement X.
The high-relief, designed by Mattia de Rossi (1684) shows Pope Clement X opening the
Holy Door during a ceremony for the Holy Year 1675.

The Popes of the Holy Years

BONIFACE VIII (1294-1303) **HOLY YEAR 1300.**
Born into an illustrious family as Benedetto Caetani in Anagni in 1235, he was ambitious and energetic, a great jurist and champion of ecclesiastic supremacy over political power. It was perhaps these characteristics that led him to declare the year 1300 as the first Holy Year in the history of the Church. The Holy Year ran from February 22, 1300 to Easter Sunday, 1301. The first Holy year was a sort of "great pardon" for everyone, a reaffirmation of the superior power of the Church, of its saving and spiritual function that can pardon any sin and open the doors to heaven. Based on the "vox populi", Boniface decided that the Holy Year would come every hundred years. Benedetto Caetani was elected pope in a Conclave which met in Naples on December 24, 1294, after the abdication of his predecessor Celestine V. As the first act of his pontificate, Boniface returned the papal residence from Naples to Rome, where he was crowned pope on January 23, 1295 with a sumptuous ceremony in St. Peter's, in the presence of King Charles II of Anjou and his son Charles Martel. Boniface VIII died on October 11, 1303. He was buried in St. Peter's in the Caetani Chapel, which he had built by Arnolfo di Cambio, guided as always by his dream of power and eternity. Subsequently his remains were transferred to the Vatican Grottoes.

CLEMENT VI (1242-1352) - *JUBILEE YEAR 1350.*
Born Pierre Roger in France in 1291. In 1349 he declared the second Jubilee in the history of the Church with the bull "Unigenitus Dei Filius", and decided to reduce to fifty the number of years between the Jubilees, following the Jewish custom of perfect numbers, taking seven by seven and the 50th year as one of pardon.
The Holy Year was opened on December 24, 1349 and concluded on December 24, 1350. Clement VI was elected pope in Avignon in May 1342 as successor to Benedict XII, and soon squandered the immense patrimony accumulated by his predecessor. Nevertheless, he had many positive traits. A good and generous man, he took the Jews under his protection when they had been accused of having spread the plague of 1348 in France. Clement VII died at Avignon on December 6, 1352.

URBAN VI (1378-1389) - *JUBILEE YEAR 1390* .(Proclaimed).
Born Bartolomeo Prignano in 1318 in Naples, then under the Angiovins. He was nominated chancellor of the Curia by Pope Gregory XI, his predecessor, who in 1377 had brought the papal seat back to Rome after a long period in Avignon. He was elected pope in 1378 by a conclave which met in Rome at the Vatican.
The only measure of religious nature that Urban took during his pontificate was that of proclaiming, with the Bull of April 8, 1389, the Third Jubilee for the year 1390, having decided to reduce the number of years between Jubilees from the Jewish 50 to 33, the age of Jesus Christ. However, Urban VI died on October 15, 1389, and did not live to see the beginning of the Holy Year, which began on December 24th of that year. He was buried in St. Peter's and his sarcophagus can now be found in the Vatican Grottoes.

BONIFACE IX *(1389-1404)* - *JUBILEE YEAR 1390* and *1400* *(Celebration)*.
At the death of pope Urban VI, the antipope Clement VII hoped to be officially recognised as pope, but the cardinals were hostile toward him and elected the Neapolitan Pietro Tomacelli to be Pope Boniface IX on November 2, 1389. His avarice led him to declare a new Jubilee in the year 1400 with the justification of the end of the century, and he used it to grant indulgences and ecclesiastical positions to anyone who would pay. It was called the Jubilee of the "Bianchi", pilgrims dressed in white robes with a red cross painted on the chest, who beat themselves with whips. The excessive flow of pilgrims to Rome and the enormous movement of people contributed dramatically to the spreading of the plague, which caused thousands of deaths. He died young on October 1, 1404 and is buried in the Vatican Grottoes in St. Peter's.

MARTIN V *(1417-1431)* - *JUBILEE YEAR 1423.*
Born Oddone Colonna in 1368 to a noble Roman family, he was elected pope in 1417 during the Council of Constance, but reached Rome only three years later, when the Roman people welcomed him as the first Roman-born pope in 135 years. He proclaimed the new Jubilee, which was celebrated from December 21, 1422 until December 24 of the following year, regaining the Jubilee interval of 33 years (representing the age of Jesus Christ) from the Jubilee Year of 1390. He introduced two novelties: a special commemorative medal and the consecrated Jubilee entrance in the Basilica of San Giovanni in Laterano, which since 1500 has been called the Holy Door. He sought to save Joan of Arc from the stake, but died suddenly in Rome on February 20, 1421. He is buried in the Basilica of San Giovanni in Laterano.

NICHOLAS V *(1447-1455)* - *JUBILEE YEAR 1450.*
Born Tommaso Parentucelli in 1397 in Sarzana, Liguria. He was a cultured and studious pope, a sharp theologian, and a passionate art collector and patron. He began the restoration of the Vatican City and the construction of many churches and monuments. In those years, the first facade of the Trevi Fountain was built. In 1450 Nicholas V celebrated the Sixth Jubilee, proclaimed with the Bull of January 1449 "Immensa et innumerabilia". It was a tragic year, however, due to two grave events: the first, when hundreds of the faithful died when the Sant'Angelo bridge collapsed under the weight of a crowd; the second, when the spread of cholera forced the pilgrims to leave Rome and the pontifical court to relocate to Fabriano. Nicholas V died in Rome on March 24, 1455. He is buried in the Vatican Grottoes.

SIXTUS IV *(1471-1484)* - *JUBILEE YEAR 1475*.
Born Francesco della Rovere in 1414 to a noble Ligurian family, he became a cardinal in 1467, and was elected pope in 1471. He succeeded Pope Paul II, who had decided that the Jubilee would be held every twenty-five years, and since then the Jubilee interval has not been altered. With the Bull of June 1473, Sixtus IV declared the Seventh Jubilee, which was held from December 1474 through Easter 1476. From that point on, the Jubilee was more meaningfully called the Holy Year. Enemy of the Medici, in 1478 he supported the Pazzi Conspiracy in Florence against the brothers Lorenzo and Giuliano de' Medici. The revolt against the Medici failed, and the members of the Pazzi family were hung from the windows of Palazzo della Signoria. Sixtus IV died on August 12, 1484 and was buried in St. Peter's in a monumental tomb designed by Antonio del Pollaiolo.

ALEXANDER VI *(1492-1503)* - **HOLY YEAR 1500.**
Born Rodrigo de Borja near Valencia in Spain in 1431, he was the nephew of Pope Callisto III Borja. He was made cardinal in 1456 and elected pope in 1492, but his lifestyle did not change. In fact, Alexander was the "Borgia Pope" par excellence, a symbol of intrigue and ruthlessness.
He led a scandalous life, fathered numerous children, including the sadly famous Cesare and Lucretia. The name of Alexander is linked to the Jubilee of 1500, which he declared with the Bull of 1499 "Inter causas multiplices". This Eighth Jubilee brought the habit of beginning and ending the Jubilee with the opening and closing of the Holy Doors of St. Peter's, San Giovanni, San Paolo and Santa Maria Maggiore. Alexander died suddenly on August 18, 1503, and was buried in the Roman church of Santa Maria in Monserrato.

CLEMENT VII *(1523-1534)* - **HOLY YEAR 1525**.
Born Giulio de' Medici in Florence in 1478, he was the illegitimate son of Giuliano de' Medici and cousin of Pope Leo X (Giovanni de' Medici), son of Lorenzo de' Medici. The papacy of Clement saw the development of the Lutheran Protest that led to the Reformation. The "protestant" Lutheran princes celebrated a definitive triumph when the Lutheran Church organised itself as State Church with the Confession of Augusta in 1530. The Jubilee, proclaimed by Clement for the year 1525 in such a climate of antagonism, was a challenge also because he resumed the practice of granting indulgences, so hated by Luther. Clement began the Holy Year on December 24, 1524 with the opening of the Holy Doors, and concluded it on the same day of 1525. He died on September 25, 1534 and was buried in Santa Maria sopra Minerva in a mausoleum designed by Antonio Sangallo.

JULIUS III *(1550-1555)* - **HOLY YEAR 1550**.
Born Giovanni Maria Ciocchi del Monte in Rome in 1487, he was elected pope on February 8, 1550. As soon as he was elected, Julius declared the Tenth Jubilee for which his predecessor Pope Paul III, who had died November 10, 1549, had issued a prior Bull of Indiction. The Jubilee was delayed until February 24, 1550, and lasted until January 6, 1551, with the opening and closing of the Holy Doors in the four Patriarchal Basilicas. During this Holy Year, Filippo Neri took the holy orders and founded the confraternity of the pilgrims', with the mission to give spiritual and material assistance to the numerous pilgrims who came to Rome. He was accused of nepotism because he had the seventeen year-old Innocenzo del Monte, a foundling adopted by his brother, nominated to be a cardinal. Julius III died on March 23, 1555 and was buried in the Vatican Grottoes.

GREGORY XIII *(1572-1582)* - **HOLY YEAR 1575**.
Born into a noble Bolognese family in 1502, Ugo Boncompagni completed his studies in Jurisprudence and taught at the University of Bologna. In 1575 Gregory XIII celebrated the Eleventh Jubilee, and on the occasion began the tradition of the walling up of the Holy Door between Holy Years, and the commemorative medallions. During the Year, more than 400,000 faithful converged on Rome from all over Europe - an extraordinary number, especially considering that there were no more than 80,000 residents of Rome. Gregory XIII built Palazzo del Quirinale, designed by Martino Longo, as a papal summer residence. It served that function until 1870. Gregory XIII died April 10, 1585 and was buried in the chapel in St. Peter's that he had built at his personal expense, according to a design by Michelangelo.

CLEMENT VIII *(1592-1605)* - ***HOLY YEAR 1600***.
*Born Ippolito Aldobrandini in Fano on February 24, 1536. He was elect-
ed pope on January 30, 1592. In 1600 he celebrated the Jubilee, declared
with the Bull of May 10, 1599. Clement decided that Carnival would not
be celebrated during the Holy Year; instead the pope did all he could to
welcome the pilgrims, committing himself to hear confession and admin-
ister Holy Communion. In February 1600, during the Holy Year, the Dominican friar Giordano Bruno, a philosopher and lecturer a the Sorbonne,
was burnt at the stake in Campo de' Fiori for heresy. He had the main altar built in St. Peter's and the Sala del Concistoro, the Sala Clementina
and the Papal Apartments built at the Vatican. He died suddenly on
March 3, 1605, while he was presiding over a session of the Tribunal of the
Inquisition. He is buried in the Basilica of Santa Maria Maggiore.*

URBAN VIII *(1623-1644)* - ***HOLY YEAR 1625***.
*Born Maffeo Barberini in 1568 in Florence, he was unanimously elected
pope on August 6, 1623. In April of the following year, he declared the Jubilee, which was celebrated in 1625 and the pilgrims who came to Rome
found the recently completed majestic facade of St. Peter's, designed by Carlo Maderno. Under his papacy many churches were restored and the facade
of San Giovanni in Laterano was completely remade. He had the Pantheon
restored and stripped the bronze which covered its roof in order to reuse it
for the twisted columns which support the enormous baldacchino (canopy)
in St. Peter's and for cannons in Castel Sant'Angelo. With regard to the discipline of the clergy, he applied the decrees of the Council of Trent and re-
inforced the Inquisition. Urban VIII died on July 29, 1644 and is buried in
the Basilica of St. Peter's. The monument in his honour is by Bernini.*

INNOCENT X *(1644-1655)* - ***HOLY YEAR 1650***.
*Born Giovanni Battista Pamphili in Rome in 1574. He was elected pope on October
4, 1644. In 1650, the Holy Year that he had declared with a Bull in May 1649, was
celebrated. Innocent made important contributions to the architectural and artistic
improvement of Rome. He was responsible for the arrangement of Piazza Navona,
with the construction of the Church of Sant'Agnese and its bell tower by Borromini,
the fountains by Bernini, and Palazzo Pamphili, which faces onto the piazza. He
had Algardi build Villa Pamphili on the Janiculum Hill, and entrusted Borromini
with the reconstruction of the Church of San Giovanni in Laterano. He showed himself to be very open to the material and spiritual needs of the weakest people, and
asked Tzar Alessio I to release the serfs. In Rome, he had the Carceri Nuove (New Prisons) rebuilt on Via Giulia. He died in 1655 and many years later was buried in the
Church of Sant'Agnese, where his nephew Camillo built a monument in his honor.*

CLEMENT X *(1670-1676)* - ***HOLY YEAR 1675***.
*Born Emilio Bonaventura Altieri in 1590 in Rome, he was an apostolic Nuncio in
Naples and then in Poland. Nominated to be a cardinal by Clement IX in 1669,
he had already turned eighty by the time he was elected pope on May 11, 1670.
Ever more concerned by the growing threat of an Islamic invasion, Clement X
sought the military support of Poland, which at the time was Christianity's bulwark
to the east, by asking its Catholic king Giovanni Sobieskj to create an alliance
against the Turks. Under the banner of this crusading spirit, the aged pope declared and celebrated the Jubilee of 1675, which was characterized by great celebrations. He tried to attract the greatest number of faithful, which were divided by
the wars in Europe, and sincerely hoped in the miracle of peace. Queen Christina
of Sweden was in Rome that year. He died on July 22, 1676 and was buried in St.
Peter's in a grandiose funeral monument built by Cardinal Paluzzi.*

INNOCENT XII *(1691-1700)* - **HOLY YEAR 1700.**
Born Antonio Pignatelli on March 13, 1615 to a noble Neapolitan family in Puglia. The conclave that proclaimed him pope on July 15, 1691 lasted five months, the longest of the year, and was characterized by power struggles among the political factions of cardinals. Innocent XII was generous and charitable to the poor. He did his best to protect the population of Rome, which had suffered through the plague, an earthquake and the flooding of the Tiber river.
Innocent finished his pontificate in the glory of the Jubilee of 1700, the year in which peace reigned in Europe and the representatives of the great powers stood united together before the Holy Doors. The "good pope" as he was known, did not see the conclusion of the Holy Year; he died on September 27, 1700.

CLEMENT XI *(1700-1721)* - **HOLY YEAR 1700** *(Closing).*
The Holy Year of 1700 was closed by the next pope, born Gian Francesco Albani, who was elected very quickly on November 23, 1700. Clement XI, a cultured pope and lover of the arts, dedicated himself to protect Rome's works of art, creating a law to defend its artistic patrimony. Elected pope with the votes of Spanish cardinals just after the death of Charles II of Spain, he maintained an ambiguous position on the War of Spanish Succession, first supporting Phillip V (1701), then, under the threat of Imperial troops which had invaded Comacchio, Charles VI of Austria (1709).
Clemente XI was pope for over twenty-one years. He died on March 19, 1721 and was buried under the floor in St. Peter's where he is remembered with a marble gravestone.

BENEDICT XIII *(1724-1730)* - **HOLY YEAR 1725**.
Born Pier Francesco Orsini at Gravina in Puglia in 1649. He was elected pope on May 29, 1724. Benedict was an ascetic, one who lived a simple, almost poor life, and had absolutely no idea of what it was to "govern". Benedict therefore occupied himself almost exclusively with the spiritual sides of his job.
He canonized San Luigi Gonzaga and San Stanislao, patron of Poland; with the Bull of June 26, 1724 "Redemptor et Dominus noster Jesus Christus" he declared the new Holy Year 1725, during which the imposing Spanish Steps, which join the piazza below with the Church of the Trinià dei Monti, were inaugurated. Benedict XIII died on February 2, 1730 and was buried in a sumptuous mausoleum in the church of Santa Maria sopra Minerva.

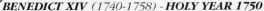

BENEDICT XIV *(1740-1758)* - **HOLY YEAR 1750**.
Born Prospero Lambertini on May 31, 1675 in Bologna. Benedict made many changes to the city, such as the restoration of the Colosseum, in which a Cross was erected. He wanted to protect the amphitheatre from continual sacking for building materials, above all travertine.
He is also credited with the continuation of papal portraits in the Basilica of San Paolo. The Jubilee of 1750 was declared in May 1749 with the Bull "Peregrinantes a Domino". Pilgrims from every part of the world arrived in Rome that year, even from the Antilles and Africa. Benedict XIV died May 3, 1758.
He was buried in St. Peter's in a sumptuous monument built by the cardinals whom he had elected, which is little suited to his simple, yet (from an apostolic point of view) towering personality.

CLEMENT XIV (1769-1774) - **HOLY YEAR 1775** (Proclamation).
Born Giovanni Vincenzo Ganganelli in Romagna in 1705. He was elected pope on May 28, 1769. Despite the compromises that accompanied his election, he carried forward among the most arduous of programs, he wanted to re-pacify the Holy See with all the Catholic leadership and restore credibility to the figure of the pope in a spirit of fraternity.
He did not succeed, in large part because he surrounded himself with treach-erous prelates who pursued their own interests, yielding to an ecclesiastical "lib-ertine" style of living, in accordance with the bad practices of the time. He died in September, 1774, after having declared the Jubilee with the Bull "Salutis nos-trae auctor".
His remains were interred in St. Peter's, then transferred by Pope Pius VII in 1802 to the church of SS. Apostoli, in a superb mausoleum built by Canova.

PIUS VI (1775-1799) - **HOLY YEAR 1775** (Celebration).
Born in Cesena in 1717 to the noble Braschi family. He was elected pope on February 15, 1775, and one of the first acts of his pontificate was the opening of the Holy Year. The Jubilee, which had been declared by his predecessor Clement XIV, began late, on February 26, and concluded on December 31, 1775. In December 1797, the French General Duphot was killed in Rome, which Napoleon used as a pretext to conquer Rome and declare the end of the temporal power of the Church. Rome was pro-claimed a republic and Pius VI was made a prisoner and deposed. He was first enclosed in a convent in Siena, then moved, in a long calvary, to Fiesole, Bologna, and in the end in the fortress of Valence, at the time under French control, where he died on August 29, 1799. In 1822 his re-mains were transferred to St. Peter's.

LEO XII (1823-1829) - **HOLY YEAR 1825**.
Born Annibale Sermattei to a noble family on August 22, 1760 in the Genga Castel in the province of Ancona. The conservative faction made him pope, against his own will, on September 28, 1823. He was a fun-damentally good man, and distributed money to the poor. He also fol-lowed a conservative economic policy, which called for the reduction of expenses and the abolition of some taxes. He had the Basilica of San Paolo rebuilt, which had been destroyed in a fire in July 1823, and re-stored the Vatican Palace, where he returned to live.
During this Jubilee, over 500,000 pilgrims visited Rome, among them many Italian and European princes. For the Holy Year, Valadier de-signed Piazza del Popolo, with a terrace set into the Pincio Hill. Leo XII died on February 10, 1829 and is buried in St. Peter's.

PIUS IX (1846-1878) - **HOLY YEAR 1875**.
Born Giovanni Maria Mastai Ferretti on May 13, 1792 in Senigallia in the Marche. In 1869, Pius IX convoked the First Vatican Council, which concluded with the proclamation of the doctrine of papal infallibility in matters of faith when the pope speaks "ex cathedra". The pope gave the order to suspend all resistance and accepted the end of his temporal reign, closing himself in the Vatican Palaces. Pius IX saw the passing of two Jubilees - in addition to this one, there was the Jubilee of 1850, which was not celebrated - but he had never opened the Holy Doors. He gave the benediction for the opening of the Holy Year, and the jubilee pardon was extended to the entire world "Urbi et Orbi". Pius IX died on February 7, 1878. His remains, deposited temporarily in St. Peter's, were interred three year's later in the Basilica of San Lorenzo fuori le Mura.

LEO XIII *(1878-1903)* - **HOLY YEAR 1900**.
Born Vincenzo Gioacchino Pecci on March 2, 1810 at Carpineto in Lazio. He was elected pope on February 20, 1878 in a conclave that lasted just 36 hours. With the 1891 encyclical "Rerum Novarum", he delineated the position of the Church regarding the social question.
With a Bull dated May 1899, Leo personally proclaimed the Holy Year 1900. In this Jubilee, the traditions and solemn ceremony were revived, including the opening of the Holy Doors, beginning with those of San Paolo, which had not been opened since 1825. There was also the exceptional event of the complete illumination, for the first time ever, of the facade and the cupola of St. Peter's by "electric light".
Leo XIII died on July 20, 1903 at age 93, and today is buried in the Church of San Giovanni in Laterano.

PIUS XI *(1922-1939)* - **HOLY YEAR 1925** *and* **1933** *(Extraordinary).*
Born Achille Ratti on May 31 1857 in Desio, near Milan. When he was elected pope on February 2, 1922, his first words expressed his willingness to resolve the Roman Question with the Italian State. In 1933, Pius XI declared and celebrated the first "Extraordinary Jubilee for the Redemption", which corresponded to the 19th centennial of the death and resurrection of Jesus Christ. The Holy Year began, with the opening of the Holy Doors in the four Basilicas, on Holy Saturday April 1, 1933 and concluded on April 2 1934. During the year there was an impressive flow of the faithful from all over the world more than two million people. Pius XI died on February 10, 1939, exactly one day before the celebration for the tenth anniversary of the signing of the Lateran Treaties. He was buried in the Vatican Grottoes.

PIUS XII *(1939-1958)* - **HOLY YEAR 1950**.
Born Eugenio Pacelli on March 2, 1876 in Rome, he graduated with a degree in theology from the Gregorian University in 1899, and was ordained in the same year.
He was unanimously elected pope on his sixty-third birthday, March 2, 1939. With the Bull "Jubilaeum Maximum" of May 1949, he declared the Jubilee of the Holy Year 1950. A new Holy Door, entirely in bronze, was made by the sculptor Vico Consorti, and for the first time the ceremonial ritual of the solemn mass marking the opening of the Jubilee was rescheduled from Christmas morning to Christmas Eve at midnight. In that year, Pius XII proclaimed the dogma of the Assumption of the Virgin Mary into Heaven. He died October 9, 1958 and is buried in the Vatican Grottoes.

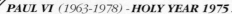

PAUL VI *(1963-1978)* - **HOLY YEAR 1975**.
Born Giovanni Battisti Montini at Concesio in Lombardy in 1897, he was ordained in 1920, and then moved to Rome where he studied at the Gregorian University. When he became pope on June 21, 1963, he followed his predecessor's vast, innovative programs. Immediately after his election, Paul VI wanted to bring an end to the Vatican II Council, begun by John XXIII, in conformity with the innovative direction and great openness with which the Council had been convened. With the Bull "Apostolorum Limina" he declared the Jubilee, which was celebrated in 1975. It was the first Holy Year in which the ceremonies of the opening and closing of the Holy Doors was televised. Paul VI died at Castel Gandolfo on August 6, 1977 and was buried in the Vatican Grottoes in a simple tomb upon which only his name is written.

JOHN PAUL II *(1978)*

EXTRAORDINARY HOLY YEAR 1983
GREAT JUBILEE OF 2000

Born Karol Wojtyla in Wadowice, Poland on May 18, 1920. He is the first Polish pope, and the first non-Italian pope in 455 years; the last was the Dutch Hadrian VI.

In 1946 he graduated with a degree in theology from the Catholic University of Krakow, and was ordained as a priest in the same year, beginning his active life as a pastor, above all among workers and the young. At just 38 years of age he was nominated to be the auxiliary bishop of Krakowa, and became an archbishop in 1967, after having actively participated in the Second Vatican Council.

In the same year, Paul VI nominated him to be a cardinal. He was elected pope on October 16, 1978, and from that day has led the Church with authority, love and dedication. John Paul II has given a vigorous impulse and a strong relevance to the ecumenical dialogue, and he has always battled for the unity of all Christians. He has showed a natural vocation for charity and he is endowed with a particular charisma, which grants him a good rapport with all human beings.

In 1979 he went to Constantinople to meet the orthodox patriarch. In 1986, he made a gesture of reconciliation by going to the Synagogue in Rome, where he preyed with the Jews, the "big brothers" of the Christians. In 1989 he received then Soviet premier Mikhail Gorbachev at the Vatican. In his twenty years as pope, Wojtyla the "missionary" has traveled 1,115,000 kilometers in 84 trips abroad, visiting more than 100 countries on every continent.

His political approach toward the East in the eighties made a substantial contribution to the fall of communism in Eastern Europe and the former Soviet Union, which was symbolically represented by the fall of the Berlin Wall in 1989.

In 1993, during his visit to Sicily, he took a hard stance against the Mafia. He continually pressures the West and the capitalistic world in general for a less frenetic consumerism and more generosity toward the third and fourth world. For the great Jubilee of 2000, he has asked the industrialized nations to cancel third world debts. His tireless, grief-ridden appeals for peace from the government of all states, belligerent or not, have earned him the title "pope of peace".

Bishop of Rome in the real sense of the word, he has made visits to the parishes of the city part of his daily routine. His papal audiences are always extremely well-attended. It was at the end of one such audience, in May 1981, that he was the victim of an attempted assassination. The whole world was shocked, then followed with trepidation as John Paul fought for his life, confronting his suffering with the same courage and Christian spirit he has shown throughout his life

Pope Wojtyla has written thirteen Encyclical letters, many of which reassert the principles of the faith, the positions of the Church on issues such as social justice, the defense of life and the Christian ethic.

In 1983 he celebrated the extraordinary Holy Year of the Redemption, which took place from March 1983 to April 22, 1984, in which the Holy Doors were opened.

With the letter "Terzio Millennium adveniente", John Paul II began the preparations for the Great Jubilee of the year 2000 and on November 29, 1998, on the first Sunday of Advent, with a solemn ceremony at St. Peter's, he began the count-down for this Holy Year, solemnly giving the Bull "Incarnationis Mysterium" to those responsible for the four Patriarchal Basilicas in Rome.

The traditional visits during the Jubilee Year

The Christian who has the fortune of celebrating the Jubilee Year in the City in which the seed transplanted from Palestine has given its benefits, will certainly follow with deep faith the traditional path, animated by the still vibrant language of the art and monuments of two millennia of Christian history.

Since the purpose of our visit is clearly religious, the interest of these pages will turn mostly to the historic events linked to the immortal monuments that we shall visit, while nonetheless emphasising their deeply meaningful artistic character.

Each one of the four patriarchal Basilicas, which constitute the basic stages of the Jubilee Pilgrimage, represents a distinctive character of the Universal Church: St. Peter's in the Vatican, standing guard over the Tomb of the first Vicar of Christ, and the See of His heirs and followers, is the clear symbol of the unitary dimension and universality of the Christian Faith.

The evangelising and missionary role of the Church could not be better represented than in the figure of St. Paul, the Apostle of the People: this, therefore, will be the main element of reflection with which we will visit the Basilica of St. Paul Outside the Walls.

How could a Catholic forget the role of Mary, Mother of God? The Basilica dedicated to her, Santa Maria Maggiore, which has an analogous role in the final pilgrimage, in the City of the Martyrs, to which the Marian Basilica is consecrated.

At last, worth of the other three Basilicas is the Patriarchal Basilica of St. John Lateran, consecrated to both Saints carrying the same name who had the fortune of living close to Christ, Cathedral of the Pope; Mother of all Churches, next to which the Roman Popes took up their see for many centuries.

The number of places prescribed as Jubilee sites has increased over the course of the centuries. From the Jubilee of 1300, in which there were only the Basilicas of St. Peter and St. Paul, the Church of St. John Lateran was added for the following Holy Year. In the third Holy Year, the Basilica of Santa Maria Maggiore joined the other patriarchal basilicas. In the Holy Year of 1575, Pope Gregory XIII added the Churches of San Sebastiano, San Lorenzo Fuori Le Mura and Santa Croce in Gerusalemme, bringing the total to seven, a sacred number. On the occasion of the extraordinary Holy Year of 1983, John Paul II added the Catacombs to the Jubilee sites in the Eternal City, for their emblematic role in the birth and early diffusion of the Church of Rome. Finally, with the Jubilee of 2000, John Paul II has inserted the Sanctuary of the Madonna of Divine Love among the traditional sites of Jubilee visits.

Saint Peter's Square and the colonnade built by Bernini.

1. *Santa Maria Maggiore.*
2. *The Basilica of San Paolo.*
3. *The Basilica of St. John Lateran.*
4. *St. Lawrence outside the Walls.*
5. *Saint Sebastian.*
6. *Santa Croce in Gerusalemme.*

The Basilica of St. Peter's

Very few States in the world can boast a vestibule like that created by St. Peter's Square; this extraordinary entrance gives the visitor a sense of serene and deep equilibrium which may indeed be described as incomparable. The perfect harmony between the square with its colonnade and the basilica crowned by the famous dome might suggest that it is the coherent work of a single talented artist. Yet the **colonnade** (1656-65) with its two curved arms was built by Gianlorenzo Bernini, one of the greatest architects of 16th-century Europe, about 50 years after the addition of the façade by Carlo Maderno

in 1614 and more than 70 years after the completion of the dome (1590). Even the pink granite **obelisk** which stands in the center, made in Egypt in the Roman epoch, and the **two fountains**, the one on the right designed in 1613 by Carlo Maderno and the other in 1677 by Carlo Fontana, were erected at different times; nonetheless Bernini succeeded in perfectly harmonizing all these different elements. Moreover Bernini himself who dedicated his life between 1657 and 1665 declared to have conceived the colonnade as a joke of proportions taken from the human body, similar in its connection with

the construction of the Basilica, to the comparison of the arms with the head.

Now let's stop at admiring the **façade**: although the excessive horizontal extension compelled Maderno to guard the sight of the magnificent *cupolone* ("huge dome") of Michelangelo, it is characterized by a sober nobility. In the centre there is the *Loggia delle Benedizioni* from where every new Pontiff is elected.

From here there is the access to the *portico*, noble place of wide dimension, masterpiece of Carlo Maderno himself. On top of the median entry, an important fragment of the Old Basilica is placed: it is the famous *mosaic of the Navicella* attributed to Giotto, representing precisely the boat of the Apostles in peril of sinking, while Christ and Saint Peter were walking on the waves. Even though his artistic interest is reduced by the

various additional touches and remakings suffered during the centuries, the work presents a great storic and documentary value since it derives from the old Basilica.

Opposite to the railing that encloses the portico, there are five grand doors following one upon the other, correspondent to as many naves that divide the inside of the Basilica. Of particular interest is the **main door** once located in the Basilica of Constantine. In fact, it dates back to 1433, year in which the sculptor Filarete of Florence ended it after twelve years of work. On the upper part, the *Redeemer* and the *Blessed Virgin* are represented both on the Throne, while the rectangles below represent *scenes of the life of Saint Peter and Saint Paul.*

The two doors that flank it as well as the one placed on the extreme left of the visitor, are locked by bronze wings made by contemporary artists. It seems particularly important

The Vatican. Aerial view.

to us to emphasize this witness of the ever lasting artistic vitality of the Basilica; worth of being admired for its characteristic is the *door* sculptured by one of the most famous artists of our age, Giacomo Manzù. It is the first door starting from the left and represents in the panels of the part facing the Portico various scenes of death. *The Death of Jesus* and the *Death of the Virgin Mary* are represented in very large dimensions compared to the ones of the other scenes, among which, there is standing out, above all, the *Death of Pope John XXIII*, and a character of great interest is also shown in the *Death in the Space*.

The *Holy Door*, which is located on the extreme right of the entry of the Portico, is usually open only in the period of the Jubilee Year by the Pope himself, who, at the end of the Ju-

bilee Year arranges to lock the door again.

Inside, the Holy Door shows *bronze wings* on which there are engraved some inscriptions related to their placing determined by Pius XII, in memory of the XXIV Jubilee Year celebrated by Pope Pacelli in 1950. Here we are *inside* the Basilica.

The visit starts from the *main aisle*, flanked by three couples of pillars with channelled *pilaster* strips, naturally of enormous dimension on which they placed very large arcades as well. Near the main door, a grand *disc of porphiry* that in the old Constantine Basilica was placed near the High Altar, stands out on the rich marble pavement, on which during Christmas night of the year 800 the Emperor Charlesmagne received the Imperial Crown from Pope Leo III.

St. Peter's façade designed by Carlo Maderno.
On pages 42 and 43, an aerial view of the St. Peter's Square and Basilica.

Inside the faces of the big two lines of niches with big statues stand among the pilaster strips. The lower ones represent *promoters of religious powers*, and precisely, on the right, Saint Teresa, Saint Vincent of Paoli, Saint Filippo Neri. while, on the left, we admire Saint Peter of Alcantara, Saint Camillo, Saint Ignazio, Saint Francis of Paola.

The arcades as well, that follow one another along the aisle, are decorated with *statues* of allegorical nature, that contribute to emphasize the solemn character of devotion of the whole atmosphere, while the interior faces of the pillars, covered with coloured marbles, show lockers with the figure of the first Popes. On the whole sculptural decoration of the main aisle, anyway, it is clearly shown out not only for its storic-artistic im-

portance but mostly for the deep devotion with which it is spread since a long time, the *bronze Statue of Saint Peter* once considered to belong to the V century. On the contrary, recent researches attributed this statue to Arnolfo di Cambio. At the centre of the Basilica, exactly on the place where the devotion of a period of two thousand years, encouraged by recent archaeologic researches, has venerated the Tomb of the Apostle, the *High Altar* is placed, on top of which the grandiose canopy of Bernini is standing, beneath the magnificent semispheric bowl of the Michaelangelesque Dome. According to the primary project of Michaelangel, the whole Basilica had to proceed from this main nucleus, with a greek cross plant, in which in other words, the lenght of the aisles had to

41

correspond to that of the limbs of the transept.

Although the validity and severity of the Michaelangelesque project, exigencies of faith suggested Paul IV, under whose pontificate Carlo Maderno concluded the construction of the Basilica to choose the so called latin cross plant with the aisles longer than the limbs of the transept, and therefore more holding. Nevertheless, such a change has not obscured the architectural and symbolic validity of the grandiose Dome, firmly settled on four powerful angular *pillars*, in which Bernini opened as many large *niches* containing statues of Saints, of colossal dimension as we have al-

ready mentioned. They are linked to the events of the relics saved in the pillars themselves and placed in the overhanging *balconies* properly embellished. So, the first pillar on the right shows the *statue of Saint Longin*: in fact, as the epigraph placed there declares, it is saved the *lance*, with which the tradition wants that the Saint represented here had hit the chest of Jesus Christ inflicting the finishing stroke.

The next pillar shows the *statue of Saint Helen,* mother of the Emperor Constantine, whom the religious research attributes the discovery of the Cross of Jesus. The precious relic coming from the Sessorian

St. Peter's Square during a Sunday morning "Angelus",
officiated by the pope from the window of his studio.

The colonnade, built by Bernini between 1656 and 1666, borders Saint Peter's Square.

Basilica was placed here by Urban VIII. The *statue of St. Veronique* is linked to one of the scenes of the Via Crucis.

The fourth pillar, at last, shows the grandiose *statue of Saint Andrew*, whose head was carried from Acaia under the pontificate of Pius II and put here as all other relics by Urban VIII. It is the moment to look over the powerful pillars, further up to the dizzy height of the **Dome**. This is supported by four colossal pendentives that constitute the elements of union between the quadrangular basis and the circular tambour decorated with circles of adequate dimension (they have, in fact, a diameter of 8 meters) in which the *Four Evangelists* are represented in mosaic.

The Dome is divided by sixteen big ribs into the same number of gores harmoniously correspondent to the huge windows beneath, decorated with grand figures in six orders

that, starting from the lunettes placed on the basis of the calotte, represent:

1) busts of *Saint Popes* and *Doctors of the Church*; 2) grandiose figures seated representing the *Redeemer*, the *blessed Virgin*, *Saint John Baptist* and other *apostles*; 3) *Angels* having various symbols, engraved in quadrilateral; 4) tondi with small head of *seraphs*; 5) Still other small heads of *seraphs* put on top of the gores.

Under the dizzy height of the dome, the Italian art has placed another splendid although extremely different interpretation of the solemn religiousness thanks to which Bernini spread his violent idea of architecture inside and outside the Basilica. Once again, we cannot do without making a significant comparison in order to give an idea of the dimension of the whole inside of the Basilica of Saint Peter: the **Canopy**, that seen from the

The bronze statue of St. Peter.

along the side aisles, the transept and the presbytery. Let's start from the *right aisle* on which, exactly like the left aisle, there are various Chapels, often linked one another through middle passages in which treasures of artistic and spiritual value are kept.

In the first Chapel of the right aisle appears clearly to our touched admiration the famous **Pietà**, made by Michaelangelo when he was just 25 years old. The deep pathos that animates the group, in which the aeternally ever young Mother and the dead Son leaning down on her arms make an indissoluble whole, reminds us that this subject was strongly felt by Michaelangelo, who in his last years had repeated it again many times, reaching always results of extremely high spirituality. On the aisle, walking toward the transept, we find one across the other the first two important funeral monuments: leaning on against the first pillar that appears at the main aisle arises the *Monument dedicated to Christine of Sweden*, one of the most famous Queens of the history. Opposite it is placed the *Monument dedicated to Pope Leo XII (1823-1829)*, beneath which there is the entrance to the *Chapel of the Relics*, of elliptical shape open at the inside of the first lateral pillar of the aisle. The Chapel is also called of

The Holy water stoup is supported by gigantic cherubs (1725).

top of the Dome seems almost a nick-nack, is 29 meters high, namely, it has the same height of a big Renaissance building.

The same style of the *Canopy* characterizes the grandiose *Chair* of Bernini style, placed on the bottom of the apse over which we shall linger over later on, at the moment, we just emphasize the harmonius correspondence between the two masterpieces that Bernini made at a distance of almost thirty years. Under the *Papal Altar*, reserved to the Pontiff, there is the **Confession**, in which two semicircular flights of steps go down toward the level of the old Constantine Basilica arisen next to the *Tomb of the Apostle* and Confessor of his faith (that's exactly the term of Confession).

Going back now at the entrance of the Basilica, let's start the "external" round going

The central nave of St. Peter's Basilica.

the *Crucifix* for the valuable medieval wooden masterpiece, representing precisely *Jesus on the Cross* attributed to the Roman artist of the thirteenth century, Pietro Cavallini.

The next *Chapel of Saint Sebastian* is so called for the mosaic with which it is decorated reproducing the *Martirium of Saint Sebastian*, taken from an altar-piece by Domenichino. At this purpose, we remind to the visitor that almost all the paintings that used to decorate the Basilica, have been moved to the Vatican Museums or to the vestries. On the place of the original works there have been placed the mosaic reproductions, made by the School of Mosaic for the Vatican. In this Chapel, there is also a modern work: it is the *Monument to Pius XI* (1922-1939), made by Pietro Canonica in 1949, decennium of the Pope's death.

On the aisle, between this chapel and the next one, we admire other two funeral monuments that remind us, one in front of the other, of a Pontiff and a famous woman of the history. It is the Sepolchrus of the XVIII century belonging to *Innocent XII* in front of which it is placed the *Monument to Countess Matilde of Canossa*, masterpiece of both storic and artistic importance. The monument was a project of Gianlorenzo Bernini, instead the statue of the Countess was sculptured by his scholar Andrea Bolgi.

A few steps away, on the right, there is the vast *Chapel of the Blessed Sacrament* in which the Holy Species are kept in a somptuous golden bronze *tabernacle* which belongs itself to Gianlorenzo Bernini. Truly, Bramante became famous just for his work of dem-

47

The tomb of St. Peter.

olishment since he died before the reconstruction had began. His first succeders were great artists, namely Raffaello and Michaelangelo. And here we are at last at the or *Gregorian Chapel* or *Chapel of Madonna del Soccorso* that took her first denomination from Pope Gregory XIII; in fact, he entrusted the construction of the Chapel to Giacomo della Porta the year next to the one of the overmentioned Reform. The other denomination is given by the small extremely worshipped painting of the XII Century coming from the Constantine Basilica representing precisely the *Madonna del Soccorso*.

Going back to the aisle, we admire, leaning on the angular pillar of the dome the *Communion of Saint Jerome*, a reproduction in mosaic of the most famous painting by Domenichino.

Let's proceed to the *right wing of the Transept* where on December 1869 Pope Pius IX was at the head of the ceremony of the opening of the Ecumenic Council Vatican I. In this wide space there are three Altars: on the right there is the *Altar of Saint Venceslao*, with the mosaic representing the Martyrdom of the Saint himself, from the painting by Angelo Caroselli; in the middle, the *Altar of the Saints Processo and Martiniano* with the altar piece in mosaic reproducing the *Martyrdom of the two Saints* Giambologna's work; on the left, there is the *Altar of Saint Erasmo*, on which the mosaic Altar-piece from a painting of the famous French painter of the XVII century, Nicholas Poussin, represents the *Martyrdom of the Saint*.

Walking along the second pillar of support of the dome, always on the right we find, opposite to another important artistic masterpiece, the *Monument in memory of Clement*

Michelangelo's Pietà.

*The Chapel of the Blessed Sacrament.
In front, Bernini's superb baldacchino (altar
canopy) during a religious celebration.*

scenographical **throne**, that bears the characteristic signs of the original art of Gianlorenzo Bernini. The throne is supported by gigantic figures of two Fathers of the Latin Church, Saint Agostino and Saint Ambrogio, and two figures of the Greek Church, Saint Atanasio and Saint Giovanni Crisostomo. The tiara and the keys. symbols of the papal authority, supported by small angels, surmont the Throne itself, concentrating the value symbolically. Above all, at last, there is standing the round window full of light in which it is dominating the polychrome figure of the pigeon-shaped *Holy Ghost* surrounded by a phantasmagoric nimbus of glorifying angels.

On the right side we can see the *Monument in memory of Urban VIII* a work of Bernini himself, although realized more than twenty years before the realization of the Chair, shows a perfect equilibrium between sculpture and architecture, that was one of the most significant merit of the artist.

Opposite there is the *Monument in memory of Paul III* (1534-1550) realized by Guglielmo della Porta who, going back to the preceding century, was placed here afterwards, exactly in order to stand close to Urban VIII Monument. From the apse, through a passage where the *Monument in memory of Alexander VIII* (1689-1691) was erected, we arrive at the *Chapel of the Column*, placed on the opposite side, symmetrically to that of *Saint Michael*. It has such a denomination thanks to a tract of column derived from the Constantine Old Basilica, on which a worshipped image of the *Blessed Virgin* is painted, placed on an Altar. As far as the artistic field is concerned, in the Chapel stands out the singular marble altarpiece in relief by Alexander Algardi, representing the *encounter between Saint Leo Magnus and Attila*. It is one of the main monuments of the Christian Middle Ages.

Proceeding toward the exit of the Basilica we note on the right the *Monument to Alexander VII*, sculpted by Bernini, on the left the *Altar of the Sacred Heart*, mosaic by C. Muccioli. On the *left wing of the transept* similarly to the right one, there are three altars: on the right the one surmonted with the mosaic altar-piece representing the *Incredulity of St. Thomas* of the neo-classic painter Vin-

XIII by Canova, in which the elegance rather cold, but extremely sober of the great neoclassic sculptor, shows with considerable similarity the spirit of his age.

Afterwards we visit the *Chapel of Saint Michael,* so called from the theme of the high altar-piece reproduced in mosaic, masterpiece of the XVII century by Guido Reni in which *Saint Michael* shows a feeling of proud vitality.

In the next passage there are placed the *Monument to Clement X* in which we notice above all the relief representing the Opening of the Holy Door, in occasion of the Jubilee Year 1675, and the altar with the altar-piece in mosaic representing *Saint Peter who revives Tabita*. From here we overlook the stately *apse* the centre of which consists of the

The interior of the Michelangelo's dome decorated by Cavalier d'Arpino.

Michelangelo's majestic dome.

The Baptismal Font.

mosaic representing the *Miracle of the cloth* undertaken by the Holy Pontiff himself.

Lying on the left wall of the Chapel there is *Pius VII Monument* (1820-1823) work of the Danish sculptor Bertel Thorvaldsen, roman of adoption. Going back to the aisle, we admire the mosaic reproduction of one of the masterpieces of the Italian Renaissance, the original of which is saved in the Vatican Picture-Gallery: the *The Transfiguration of Christ* that Raffaello could not complete because of his death.

The passage that takes to the next Chapel shows, on the right, the *Monument in memory of Leo XI* (1605) work of the well-known Alessandro Algardi. In front there is the *Monument in honour of Innocent XI* (1767-1689) in which the French sculptor Pietro Monnot, shows clear classic traces, in the most rigid and cultured interpretation characteristic of his country.

We now admire the *Chapel of the Chorus* that together with that of the Blessed Sacrament, in front of which it is placed on the right aisle, is the widest of the Basilica. The altar-piece on the altar represents the *Immaculate Conception*, following the original of Pietro Bianchi, while the ceiling is decorated with golden stuccoes of valuable make. In the passage on the aisle, two monuments built in two distant stages: on the right there is in fact one of the few works of our century that are placed in Saint Peter's Basilica, the *Monument in memory of Pius X* (1903-1914), built in 1923 in accordance with the project of the architect Di Fausto; opposite, an artistic jewel of the Basilica the *Monument in memory of Innocent VIII* (1484-92) by Pollaiolo, already standing in the old Basilica.

The *Chapel of the Presentation* which has such a denomination for the altar-piece on the main altar, with the *Presentation of the Blessed Virgin at the Templum*, taken from the painting of the XVII century by Giovanni Romanelli. Nevertheless, for the believers, it is mostly reason of emotion the incorrupt *body of Pius X* kept in the crystal and golden bronze urn underneath the altar.

On the right wall there is a recent artistic witness: the grandiose bronze relief of the sculptor Emilio Greco, representing *Pope John*

cenzo Camuccini; in the centre there is standing the altar consacrated to the *Saints Simon and Giuda*, of which it guards the Relics, with the mosaic reproducing *St. Joseph*, belonging to Achille Funi; on the left the altar surmonted by the *St. Peter Crucifixion* taken from the baroque painting by Guido Reni.

The passage that brings to the left aisle shows the *Altar of Anania and Saffira* or *Altar of the Lye*. Opposite, underneath the cold neoclassic work of Pietro Tenerani, representing *Pius VIII Monument* (1829-1830) there is the door that takes to the Sacristies and to the Treasury of Saint Peter.

On the *left aisle*, there is the grand *Clementine Chapel* or *Chapel of Saint Gregory Magnus*. Its first denomination derives from Pope Clement VIII, under whom it was built by Giacomo della Porta. The main altar, in which the *remains of Saint Gregory Magnus* are venerated, is sormounted by the altar piece in

The Chair of St. Peter, a theatrical work by Bernini in gilded bronze.

XXIII while visiting the prisoners in which it is reminded one of the most touching moments of the pontificate of that beloved Pastor. On the left, at last, *Benedict XV Monument* (1914-1922), work of Pietro Canonica.

The next passage in the aisle shows us the *Monument to Maria Clementina Sobieski* (1702-1735) of typical XVIII century elegance, work of Pietro Bracci. Opposite there is the marvellous *funeral stele of the late Stuarts* respectively husband and sons of Sobieski, one of the masterpieces of Antonio Canova

Our last leg inside the Basilica is at the *Chapel of the Baptistery*, at the centre of which there is the *Baptismal Font* of red porphiry characteristic of the classic age, completed in the XVIII century by Carlo Fontana with a new bronze tipically rococò composition, rich of volutes and putti, culminating in the *Agnus Dei*. In character with the destination of the Chapel there are the altar-pieces among which the *Baptism of Christ* made by Carlo Maratta.

TREASURY OF SAINT PETER'S

At the end of our visit to the Basilica, let's climb to the left nave up to the Monument in memory of Pius VIII, under which there is the access to the *Sacristies* full of rich furnishings and storic memories that would be enough to value any great Cathedral.

It is a series of rooms placed in a small independent building connected with the group of the Basilica by two arches across the street. On the right of the access, we stop running through the catalogue of 147 Popes buried in Saint Peter, from the Prince of the Apostles to John-Paul I.

After having gone through a vestibule and a corridor, we enter the *main or public Sacristy* embellished with eight columns from the sumptuous Villa of the Roman Emperor Adri-

The Cross of Justinian II (IV sec.)

an (II Century A.C.) near Tivoli. Among the adjacent rooms we remember most of all the *Chapel* that opens on the *Sacristy of the benefited clerics*, with the Donatello *ciborium* the famous sculptor of Florence who was one of the promotors of the Italian and European Renaissance, at the dawning of the XV century and with the venerated image of the *Madonna della Febbre (Our Lady of the Fever)* of the painter from Siena belonging to the XIV century, Lippo Memmi. Both the works used to decorate the pre-existent Constantine old Basilica.

From the Sacristy of the Benefited there is the entry to the nine rooms that guard the *Treasure*. There is a great number of valuable shown, precedently piled the age of Constantine (IV century) the Basilica of Saint Peter had received considerable grants, many of which thanks to the Emperor himself. Thanks to the generosity of the beneficiaries, in the next centuries although violent pillages have occurred the Treasury was strongly re-established, and even little by little enriched. Among the principal occasion of new abundant grants, we recall the first Jubilee, celebrated in 1300; naturally, the successive Jubilee Years give new grants to the collection of gifts kept here. Because of the succession of the spoliations, the valuables that we may admire go back more or less to the last two centuries. We shall not miss, anyway, to point out the few ones escaped to the pillages of the precedent centuries.

Room I - There are a *red cope* with *tiara* decorated with stones (XVIII century) destined to cover the venerated Saint Peter's statue of bronze, placed in the middle nave of the Basilica, in occasion of the solemn festivities; the so-called *Chalice Stuart*, itself belonging to the XVIII century, in gold and silver with 130 mounted brilliants.

Room II - There are exposed some of the

St. Peter's treasury. The tomb of Sixtus IV by Pollaiolo.

most precious works, among which the *Crux Vaticana* (*Vatican Cross*) covered with silver leather and precious stones, containing fragments of the real Cross; the *Dalmatix* (liturgic vestment) erroneously called of Charlemagne, since it belongs to a later age, more or less around the XI century according to some scholars, and around the XIV century according to others; numerous precious *shrines*.

Room III is dominated by the *bronze monument to Sixtus IV* (1471-84), a masterpiece by Antonio del Pollaiolo. In *Room IV* is the 14th-century *frame of Veronica* which used to hold the precious relic pressed between two sheets of glass.

In *Room V* the visitor can see *copper spheres* used as hand-warmers in the chilly sacristies, as well as a collection of *precious chalices* and *reliquaries*.

In *Room VI*, a vast collection of *candelabra* is exhibited. The small room that forms the corridor contains large sacred codices.

Room VII contains a model of one of the *worshipping angels*, made in clay and cast in bronze by Bernini for the Chapel of the Sacrament. *Room VIII* displays a collection of vestments, sacred objects and votive jewels donated to the pontiffs by the faithful from all over the world.

In *Room IX* contains an example of paleo-Christian sculpture, the *sarcophagus of Junius Bassus* (4th century).

THE SACRED GROTTOES

To visit the impressive remains of the old basilica built in the age of Constantine and which stood for about 1,200 years, one must go underground to the crypt. In the course of the rebuilding an effort was made to leave the ground-plan as intact as possible by constructing the new basilica on a higher level; consequently the existing subterranean pas-

Sacred Grottoes. Mosaic from the Constantinian Basilica portraying a swan (the symbol of love).

sages correspond to the ancient Constantinian building, with a slight difference in level. The sober and solemn complex of the Sacred Grottoes, reached down a flight of steps beneath the pillar of St. Longinus near the basilica's main altar, consists of two separate parts. The **New Grottoes** correspond to the transept above, and are the starting point for a semicircular ambulatory from which smaller ambulatories radiate to the four oratories. These correspond to the respective piers supporting the dome to whose saints they are also dedicated, and to three chapels. Beneath the central nave are the so-called **Old Grottoes**, a large space likewise divided into aisles by two long rows of low, powerful pilasters.

Along the walls and between the vast pilasters separating the three aisles, are a series of tombs of popes, (including those of Boniface VIII by Arnolfo di Cambio and of John Paul I, the last pope to be buried here after a pontificate of only 33 days) and of cardinals, bishops, kings and queens, while at the end of the aisles are some valuable works of art.

In the center of the ambulatory is the *Clementine Chapel*, whose precious malachite altar houses the ancient, unpretentious masonry altar, built by Saint Gregory the Great (590-604) above the one indicated as the Apostle's burial place from the earliest centuries. Important archaeological excavations of the underlying necropolis in the 1950's and 60's have significantly confirmed the ancient tradition that "Mass was celebrated over the body of Blessed Peter".

Opposite this chapel is a simple urn, the *tomb of Pius XII* (1939-1958), set as close as possible to the first Vicar of Christ in accordance with the pope's own wishes.

The kneeling *statue of Pius VI*, the work of Antonio Canova but which was completed by Adam Tadolini (1822), formerly stood on the level of the Confessio but has been transferred to the end of the central nave.

At the end of the side aisles are tombs of great historical and artistic importance: the *tomb of the Emperor Otto II*, a paleo-Christian sarcophagus and the *tomb of Nicholas III*, from the 4th century.

The exit from the Grottoes is located near the ticket office for the visit to the dome.

THE VISIT TO THE DOME

The entrance to the dome is located on the right of the portico of the basilica. After taking the elevator for part of the way, to the height of the central nave (about 45 meters), the visitor reaches the vast terrace above the nave itself. Above, the massive dome soars to a height of a good 92 meters, surrounded by a series of 10 lesser cupolas. Nothing could be more enchanting and picturesque than the spectacle offered from the terrace; but the spreading panorama beneath the parapet with

Sacred Grottoes. St. Peter preaching to the Romans. Mosaic from the Constantinian Basilica (IV secolo).

A religious ceremony in the Sistine Chapel with the Pope and cardinals.

Panoramic view from the dome of St. Peter's.

a view of the city marked by the winding ribbon of the Tiber is equally spell-binding.

From the base of the dome the subsequent and even more interesting phase of the ascent begins. First of all we will pause to observe the interior of the Basilicafrom the height of the ambulatory encircling the first interior entablature of the dome beneath the windows. While the colossal works we admired from the ground seemed real miniatures; from here, the figures of the saints and angels decorating the dome look gigantic.

The climb continues up steps and winding staircases of different gradients and sizes squeezed between impressively curving walls, until we finally reach the loggia around the lantern from which we can admire a second and even more extensive view of the city.

The Confession. In the background, the papal altar with the apse (XIII century), dominated by the triumphal arch (V century).

ite. The walls of the building were damaged by the 1823 fire, but fortunately, enough of the mosaics survived to allow a very delicate work of restoration. In the middle, in a large circle, the bust of Christ is represented in a blessing pose. Above, the symbols of the four Evangelists hang over the golden base, while two worshipping Angels kneel beside the medallion of Jesus, and the 24 Men of the Apocalypse offer their crowns.

Climbing a few stairs we reach the rather high TRANSEPT, which was partly saved from the fire, and which contains the two most shining jewels of art and devotion of the Basilica: the ciborium and the apse. The CIBORIUM was

made by Arnolfo di Cambio, with the cooperation, clearly shown in the cartouche engraved on the work, of Pietro Cavallini, another great representative of 12th century Roman art, whose frescoes in the main nave were unfortunately lost. The ogival arches are supported by columns, which have ancient capitals of golden leaf-shaped marble, engraved with various designs. The angular niches hold valuable statues of the saint, while reliefs of biblical scenes decorate the pinnacles. The *canopy* covering the simple Papal Altar is made of porphyry and white marble, decorated with vine branches in golden copper. It stands on top of the marble area where the Christians venerate the remains of the Apostle. To the right of the canopy there is a beautiful candelabrum for the Easter candle, a 12th century work by Peter Vassalletto and Nicolò dell'Angelo, in which the classic elements appear mixed with motifs of clearly Saracen influence.

Before going on toward the grandiose, sparkling apse mosaic at the end of the Basilica, we stop to observe the TRANSEPT, characterised by a group of twenty-four Corinthian pillars of purple marble, upon which stands a series of *mosaic medallions representing the images of the Popes.* The rich ceiling of golden arabesques on a blue and green background spans from the es-

cutcheon of the Basilica and to the medallions of the popes under whom the Basilica was restored. In the transept we admire some great altarpieces, including *St. Paul's Conversion to Christianity* by the 19th century painter Vincenzo Camuccini. There are also Four Chapels, among which the most interesting is the CHAPEL OF THE SACRAMENT, which escaped the fire. It is named for the BLESSED SACRAMENT, the centre of the liturgical life of the Church. The Chapel was built by Carlo Maderno, the architect belonging to the famous family of artists which included Stefano Maderno. He made the *statue of St. Brigida* in the Chapel. On the altar there is the 14th century *wooden crucifix* with which St.

The interior of the Basilica of St. Paul.

The Basilica of St. Paul. Christ Pantocreator. Detail of the mosaic in the apse.

Brigida spoke, once wrongly attributed to Pietro Cavallini, probably because the great artist was buried in the Chapel.

Finally, we stop in front of the APSE MOSAIC, made by the 13th century Venetian artists for Pope Honorius III, who is represented in quite small scale among four Apostles, under the image of the blessing Jesus. To the side is a cross decorated with Symbols of the Passion, with two Angels and twelve Apostles and Saints, whose images are intermingled with decorating palms. Finally, against the apse there is the papal Chair made of white marble with precious golden bronze decorations, and marvellous polychrome pavement made of valuable marble.

Going out from the right wing of the transept, we find a small complex of rooms and Chapels which lead to the CLOISTER, one of the most suggestive in Rome. In its restrained but perfect dimensions, it is a real masterpiece: pairs of small columns of different styles (smooth, with various spirals, octagonal, white, with polychrome inlays in mosaic) support a series of small round arches, while a long inscription in blue letters runs along a golden base, which clearly outlines the role of the cloister in each Monastic construction. There are also the names of the Abbots who took care of the design, entrusted to Vassalletto and the greatest 13th century Roman Marble makers.

The Cosmatesque Cloister by Vassalletto.

Passing through the sacristy and the Gregorian Room, we go out on the back of the apse, on the Via Ostiense, where stands out the heavy mass of the Bell Tower, designed by Luigi Poletti for the 19th century reconstruction of the Basilica. Although it has grandiose dimensions (it is almost 70 meters high), it does not suit the linear style of the rest of the building because of the rather inharmonious succession of the different styles of its five levels. On the side of Via Ostiense there is the large closed Abbey, See of the Benedictine Friars, who, since the high Middle Ages, have the duty of guarding the cult place, sacred to St. Paul's grave.

Detail of the twisted columns in the cloister.

The Basilica of Santa Maria Maggiore

The apse mosaic by Iacopo Torriti (XIII century).

The most ancient and greatest among the Basilicas dedicated to the cult of the Virgin Mary could not fail to be one of the fundamental steps of the Jubilee pilgrimage. Although it cannot be verified that it is the Liberian Basilica, built in 352 under Pope Liberium after a dream contemporarily appeared both to the Pope himself and to a patrician, its origins are undeniably ancient: the construction dates back at least as far as Pope Sixtus III, who built a church here to celebrate the end of the Efeso Council, which in 431 had solemny conferred upon the Blessed Virgin the title of Mother of God, thereby founding the vibrant Cult of Mary.

Although the current building follows the original structure, it shows traces of various enlargements, additions, embellishments made over the course of the centuries. The soberly scenographic *façade*, by Ferdinando Fuga, has clearly 18th century characteristics. The late Romanesque BELL-TOWER (14th century), with its characteristic pyramidal peak, stands 75 meters high, the tallest in Rome.

Before we enter the Basilica, let's stop to admire the beautiful Corinthian column made of cipolino marble, brought here by Paul V from the Constantine Basilica (better known as the Basilica of Massenzio), near the Colosseum. There is an elegant fountain in the foreground.

The *Portico* features five large architraved openings and five doors, among which the first on the left is the *Holy Door* (opening formalities are the same as for the Holy Doors at St. Peter's and St. Paul's). From the left we ascend to the *Loggia*, which is positioned against the original façade of the Basilica and the valuable mosaics that date back to the late 13th century.

The *interior* of the Basilica, divided into three naves, appears vast and harmonious. The very ample MAIN NAVE, with a rich Renaissance ceiling and splendid 12th century Cosmatesque pavement is flanked by a doubled line of huge monolithic columns on whose elegant Ionic capitals stands the sober entablature. Above are thirty-six panels dating back to the 5th century, represent-

Detail of the apse mosaic (lower section). Mary lying across the coffin.

68

The Basilica of Santa Maria Maggiore. Aerial view.

ing biblical episodes. These are very important examples of early Christian art. However, the supreme example of art and history in the Basilica is the gorgeous TRIUMPHAL ARCH that stands at the end of the nave. At the peak of the arch is the enthroned Redeemer; to the left are the Annunciation, the Epiphany, the Slaughter of the Innocents, and Jerusalem; on the right are the Presentation to the Temple, the Flight into Egypt, the three Magi in front of Herod, and Bethlehem. All the evangelical scenes represented here have the same purpose: praising the central role of Mary. Underneath the Arch is a rich CANOPY, made by the same artist who did the façade, Ferdinando Fuga. From an artistic point of view, its great dimension and wavy lines serve as elements that disturb the clear geometry of the interior. The work rises on the HIGH ALTAR, in front of which

there is the crypt of the Confession. Here the precious *relics of the Crib* are guarded: five pieces of the manger which held held the infant Jesus, which devoted Christians for the last two millennia have adored. The humble wood has been contained into a precious silver urn made at the beginning of the 19th century by Luigi Valadier, the famous Roman architect who designed, among the other things, Piazza del Popolo.

Finally, on the other side of the High Altar we admire the real apotheosis of the mosaic decoration that is the artistic highlight of this Basilica: the calotte of the apse, completely covered by a grandiose mosaic by Jacopo Torriti, dated 1295, celebrating the TRIUMPH OF MARY: Jesus crowns his Mother, who is sitting like him on the Throne while a double row of Angels and SAINTS observes the scene from the sides.

The Basilica of Santa Maria Maggiore during a religious service.

After having admired the entire mosaic cycle, let's return to the entrance in order to start an orderly tour of the side naves and the transept. On the RIGHT AISLE, there is first of all the CHAPEL OF THE BAPTISTRY, by Flaminio Ponzio (1605), while the porphyry Baptismal font is an 19th century work by Luigi Valadier. From the Baptistry, we walk to the adjacent sacristy by Flaminio Ponzio, where another two chapels stand out.

The second Chapel in the right nave, the CHAPEL OF THE RELICS, was built by Ferdinando Fuga (who also designed the façadeand of the canopy). The grandiose Sistine Chapel in the right wing of the transept was designed by the architect Domenico Fontana in the second half of the 16th century for Pope Sixtus V, who had expressed a desire to be buried here. The chapel was dedicated in the name of the pope, who completely changed the urbanistic aspect of Rome. Since the return of the popes from the Avignonese exile two centuries earlier, the city

had been enriched and embellished considerably by beautiful churches and grandiose buildings, but it had retained its web of medieval streets. Thanks to the work of Domenico Fontana, Sixtus V changed the aspect of the city and earned himself a place in the history. The architect therefore dedicated this Greek-cross shaped Chapel, surmounted by a frescoed dome, with a High Altar and a late 16th century ciborium in the shape of a small temple. Both the monument in memory of Sixtus V and that of St. Pius V, the Pope under whom the Lepanto war (1571) was fought, were built by Domenico Fontana.

Let's continue our visit to the venerable Basilica of the Blessed Virgin Mary by admiring the Tomb of the Cardinal Consalvo Rodriguez at the base of the right nave, a typical gothic monument built by Giovanni di Cosma at the end of the 13th Century.

After walking through the main aisle at the height of the Confession, we can cross to the left

To the right. The baldacchino (alter canopy) by Ferdinando Fuga (XVIII century).

wing of the transept and the symmetrical counterpart to the Sistine Chapel, the PAOLINA CHAPEL, named after Pope Paul V, who is buried there. It was built by the architect Flaminio Ponzio. Pope Paul V called on Maderno to build the façade of St. Peter's in the Vatican, upon which the name of the Pontiff stands out in capital letters, in the gigantic dedicatory inscription. The Chapel is also called *"Borghese"* after the famous Roman family to whom the Pope belonged.

In front of the *Tomb of Paul V* (1605-1624), there is the *Tomb of Clement VIII Aldobrandini* (1592-1605), his predecessor (between the two of them there was the very brief pontificate of the Medici Pope Leo XI, of the famous Florentine family, which lasted only a few mouths). Both the monuments were planned by the Architect of the Chapel, Flaminio Ponzio, who gave his masterpiece a character of splendid sumptuousness: the very rich altar decorated with agates, lapis-lazuli, jaspers and amethysts is the work of Pompeo Targoni, opon which there is one of the most venerated images among the countless ones guarded in the Roman churches: la *Madonna col Bambino* (Madonna and Child) that a religious tradition attributes to the evangelist St. Luca. In reality, the work goes back to the 11th century, more than 1000 years after the period in which the Evangelist lived. The precious painting is surrounded by a 17th century crown of angels by Camillo Mariani, who also made the bronze angels of the frontispiece, while the marble relief of the same frontispiece representing *Pope Liberium who outlines the project of the Basilica*, is by Maderno.

The frescoes that decorate the walls and the ceiling of the chapel, made by artists such as Cavalier d'Arpino, Cigoli, Lanfranco, and most of all, Guido Reni, one of the most representative painters of his age are of fundamental importance to knowledge about Roman painting in the baroque period. The Chapels that face the left nave, although less rich, are also worthy of interest: although attributed to Giacomo Della Porta (1565-1573), the noble, organic design of the Sforza Chapel corroborates the hypothesis that it was designed by Michelangelo, as were many other works by that architect.

Leaving the Basilica via the apse, we can admire the *apse façade*, finished around 1670 by Carlo Rainaldi. The undoubtedly scenographic result corresponds to the noble majesty of the Basilica, perhaps better than the main façade made by Fuga.

To the left: Santa Maria Maggiore, the Chapel of the Holiest Sacrament, also called the Sistine Chapel.

The façade of the Basilica of Santa Maria Maggiore. A close view of the Corinthian column brought here from the Basilica of Maxentius by Pope Paul V.

The Pauline Chapel, with the altar to the Virgin by P. Targoni (1600).

St. John. The tabernacle.

St. John Lateran, on the vault by Filippo Carcani.

At the end of the quick round of the aisles, let's stop at the GROSS-VAULT, which has also been completely restored several decades before the aisles. In fact, the reconstruction was made by Giacomo della Porta under the pontificate of Clement VIII, between 1597 and 1601, almost fifty years before that realised by Borromini.

In the middle stands the valuable late-Gothic TABERNACLE that was built in 1367 under Pope Urban V by the elegant Sienese artist Giovanni di Stefano. It is decorated with twelve fresco panels from the period by the painter Barna di Siena and retouched in the following century by Antoniazzo Romano. The Good Shepherd, the Crucifixion, the Blessed Virgin, and numerous Saints are represented. The *golden silver busts representing St. Peter and St. Paul* kept in the upper part, contain the venerable relics of the two Apostles.

The *papal altar* below was remade in 1851 in

white marble with small columns decorated with mosaic. It contains inside the unpolished *wooden table* upon which, according to tradition, all the first Popes once officiated, from St. Peter to St. Sylvester I (4th century).

The two wings of the transept are decorated on the sides of the walls with eight wide frescoes made by the famous Cavalier d'Arpino and his school around 1600, representing episodes related to the story and tradition of the Constantinian foundation of the Basilica, besides other frescoes representing Saints, Apostles and various scenes. In the ample, luminous hall, there are a few precious artworks. First amongthem, the solemn ALTAR OF THE BLESSED SACRAMENT, on the head of the *left wing* of the transept, surmounted by a grandiose triangular tympanum supported by four enormous channelled Corinthian columns, in golden bronze, brought from a Roman monumental building. The bronze *Tabernacle*, decorated with precious stones and held by two pairs of ancient green marble columns, is the work of Peter Targone. It is surmounted by bronze relief of Ambrogio Buonvicino. representing the *Last Supper*, behind which there is a fragment made of cedar wood, which according to tradition, belongs to the table on which Jesus and his Apostles had supper together for the last time. The whole thing is crowned with a fresco of grandiose dimensions, full of light, by Cavalier d'Arpino, representing a triumphal *Ascension*.

To the right of the Altar, we admire the CHAPEL OF THE CHORUS OR COLUMN, built in 1625 by Girolamo Rainaldi on behalf of Prince Colonna who wished in this manner to honour the memory of his wife, Lucrezia Tomacelli. Next to the Chapel there is the *Monument in memory of Leo*

St. John. The cloister.

XIII (1878-1903), the work of Giulio Tadolini.

The APSE, redone under the pontificate of Leo XIII (1884), enlarged the shape of the old Basilica, and has been decorated using the pre-existing mosaics that Jacopo Torriti and Jacopo da Camerino realised at the end of the 13th century, making use of, on the their turn, fragments of the original Constantinian mosaics. The last ones are: the *figure of the Redeemer* at half bust, placed on the upper part of the scene, and the *river Jordan*, with its usual figuration, that flows toward the lower part. Underneath, alternating with the luminous lancet windows, nine figures representing the Apostles make a celestial wing. It is interesting to notice that on the bottom of two of them, the small figures of Franciscan artists to whom the work belongs are shown with their work tools (hammer, compasses, square). Underneath, at last, is the *Papal Chair* made with precious marbles and decorated with splendid mosaics, which in this Basilica, the Cathedral of Rome, assumes the role of bishop's throne.

On the RIGHT WING OF THE TRANSEPT it is the *Monument in memory of Innocent III* (1198-1216), the great Medieval Pope, built by Giuseppe Lucchetti (1891) for Leo XIII. At the entrance we admire a *baroque organ* made by Luca Blasi from Perugia, decorated with precious small musician angels in gilded wood. Beside the CHAPEL OF THE CRUCIFIX is a statue representing Pope Boniface IX (1398-1404). The *Crucifix* that gives the chapel its name dates to the 18th century.

After the end of the visit to the Basilica, a door that opens between the left aisle and the wing of the transept, leads to an airy CLOISTER made by famous Roman marble sculptors of the 13th century, the Vassalletto family, who also made the cloister of the St. Paul's Basilica.

The Scala Santa. The Sancta Sanctorum.

St. John. The canopy and the papal altar.

Inside the Basilica, from the opposite right wing of the transept, through a door that opens under the baroque organ, we go out to ST. JOHN LATERAN SQUARE. The *side view* of the Basilica is particularly interesting. It is set on two lines of five arcades, according to the project of Domenico Fontana, going back to the end of the 16th century, while the twin bell towers stand out at the sides of the LOGGIA OF THE BLESSINGS, which is represented in the famous fresco by Giotto of the Proclamation of the first Jubilee date to the 11th century.

In the middle of the square stands an Egyptian red granite obelisk, the highest in Rome (47 meters including the base), brought from Thebes and placed here in 1588 by Domenico Fontana himself.

On the left as you exit the Basilica, there rises the separate building of the BAPTISTERY of St. John, also built during the Constantinian period. Redone during the following century, it successively suffered various restorations up to the one that took place in 1637 under Urban VIII. The in-

side is characteristic and may be considered the prototype of the Christian Baptisteries.

Among these religious places of great interest, there is also the SCALA SANTA (Holy Staircase) that faces the square of St. John Lateran.

The actual construction was made by Domenico Fontana (1585-1590) on a spot of the "Patriarchy", which belonged to the Sancta Sanctorum, the ancient private Chapel of the Popes. While the part of the ancient construction corresponding to the Lateran Palace was almost completely demolished when Pope Sixtus V had Domenico Fontana preserve two of the most important and venerated parts of the ancient "Patriarchy" in this new building. It was the renamed the "Sancta Sanctorum" and the Holy Staircase that the religious tradition identifies with that of the Praetorium of Pilate in Jerusalem that Jesus had covered many times during the Passion.

Around the year 335, the Empress St. Helen, mother of Constantine, although almost eighty years old, wanted to go to Jerusalem to find the relics of the Passion of Christ, especially the Cross of His sacrifice. Her zeal was crowned with success: the Empress brought with her a fragment of the Cross of the Redeemer and that of the one of His companions in pain, as well as other important relics of the Passion. Among them, according to the tradition, there was the SCALA SANTA (Holy Staircase) that therefore, over the course of centuries, has been the object of deep devotion. The staircase has twenty-eight marble steps, recovered with wood for protection, while small glass sheets cover some spots that are considered to be a trail of Christ's blood. Both the Holy Staircase that the Christians climb on their knees and the four lateral stairs end in front of one of the most venerable monuments of history and art of the Medieval Ages, the SANCTA SANCTORUM, or *Chapel of St. Lawrence*, come to us with the changes made under Pope Nicholas III in the last years of the 13th century. It retains numerous important features of decorative art, mostly the splendid mosaic flooring and frescoes of the school of the major painters of the 13th century, Cimabue of Florence and the Roman Pietro Cavallini. Thanks to these basic works of art, this Chapel has been called "the Sistine of the Medieval Age"; but the attention and the emotions of the visitor concentrate mostly in the famous *table of the Redeemer*, a precious icon that has been dated to the 6th century.

To the left, the interior of the Baptistry.
To the right, the Scala Santa.

The Catacombs

The name "Catacombs" dates back almost to the 9th century AD, and indicates the underground places of burial of the first Christians. The word, which means "near the ravine", comes from an area near the Appian Way, where a famous and honoured burial ground stands. The first Christians called them "cemeteries", namely "places of rest", a name that shows poetically the faith in the resurrection of the body, such as that of Jesus.

New discoveries have recently come to light; but what can be visited remains essentially that which was discovered by Bosio and De Rossi. The exigencies of space force us to limit our choice to three discoveries among the most famous and easily accessible: the Catacombs of Saint Sebastian (where there still is the depression "ad catacumbas" "catacomb-shaped" that has given the name to all other Paleo-Christian cemeteries) and the Catacombs of St. Callisto on the Appian Way, and the Catacombs of Domitilla, near Via Ardeatina.

Before starting the description, we think right to give a general view of the structure of all three Catacombs. They are formed by a series of long and narrow crossing galleries with strata laying one upon the other. This is mostly due to the necessity of concentrating the burials of a growing number of Christians in the quite limited areas granted for burial. It was necessary to save space by any means available: the galleries on whose walls the Christians used to be buried, originally two meters in height, were successively deepened. Therefore, the most ancient tombs are those standing nearest the top, as other galleries were successively excavated at a lower level. The prevalent type of tomb is the loculus, a rectangular cavity excavated in the side wall of the gallery and closed by marble slabs and tiles upon which, in many cases, the Christians engraved or painted short inscriptions and symbolic designs commemorating the dead.

Usually five levels of loculi are laid one upon the other, but the very deep galleries can reach twelve levels.

Here and there we see the so-called "arcosoli" tombs surmounted by an arc, which evidently emphasised the importance of those buried there. Often the lunette under the arch was painted or decorated with a mosaic; while the tomb could be made of a marble sarcophagus with relief decorations. Tombs of this kind were not destined only to differentiate the dead of various social levels; those who distinguished themselves by the sanctity of their lives were honoured here as well. In the first centuries of Christianity, noble and plebeian citizens, rich and poor, masters and former-slaves were buried in the loculi one next to the other, without any difference, in application of the Christian principle of the equality of men before God, of whom we all are sons, without any differentiation.

To allow space for the Christians who came to pray at the tombs of the most venerated Martyrs' crypts or cubiculi, real oratories were opened up in the 4th century, after the liberalisation of the Christian religion proclaimed by Constantine. Most of all, it was Pope Damaso who in the second half of that century endowed the catacombs with numerous, accurate marble inscription of the circumstances of martyrdom.

Above, the Catacombs of San Sebastiano. The Three Mausoleums. To the right, the ceiling of the Three Mausoleums decorated with stucco.

The Catacombs and the Basilica of St. Sebastian

The cemetery on the Appian Way which commemorates the martyrdom St. Sebastian (and contains the martyr's tomb), is probably the mostly well known in the Christian world. It was the only one to remain always accessible over the course of the centuries, and gave its name "catacomb" to all similar burial places. A 4th century Basilica dedicated to the saint, built at the entrance and almost completely renovated in the 17th century, will be visited briefly at the end of our subterranean tour.

The Catacomb is made up of four floors of galleries, of which we will visit the second one, where the *Crypt of St. Sebastian* stands, restored in modern times. The tomb of the Martyr, a soldier of Diocletian killed by his fellow soldiers with the well-known execution by arrows, was mistaken with those of the other faithful citizens; only later was it isolated, and altar put in place, making it a Confession, namely where a place dedicated to the religion of a Confessor of the faith. In 18th century a bust of St. Sebastian, attributed to Bernini, was placed here. The singular element that gives the Catacombs of St. Sebastian an unmistakable character is an area rediscovered studied between 1915 and 1933, and baptised by its discoverer, P. Styger, with the name of Triclia, namely the place destined to the celebration of funeral banquets, according to a pagan tradition in the first centuries of Christianity. The particular importance given to this underground area is connected with the fact that for a short period it welcomed the bodies of the Sts. Peter and Paul, probably in the second half of the 3rd century. In fact, numerous burials of Christians into adjacent loculi belong to this period, evidently because of the vicinity of the most venerated remains of the two Apostles. The place of the temporary burial of these remains was probably marked by a chair, whose fragments are still visible on the background wall. Among the surrounding mausoleums, the pictorial decoration dedicated to M. Clodius Hermes is of special interest; next to it there is a particularly interesting

sepulchre with fine stucco decorations.

From the Triclia, through the sacristy we reach an ambulatory that corresponds to the apse, used nowadays as museum for several very important collections of epigraphs and a series of plastic models of considerable interest, representing the TRICLIA, the most important graves and the original basilica of Constantine age. This leads to the so-called Platonia, the construction adjoining the Basilica, which was once thought to be the place of the temporary burial of Sts. Peter and Paul.

Going back to the Basilica, let's stop to admire the solemn interior with its unique aisle. On the right there is the Chapel of the Relics in which one of the arrows of St. Sebastian's martyrdom is kept, along with the stone with marks that the religion has identified with those left by Jesus when he miraculously appeared before St. Peter on his way out of Rome to escape his imminent persecution. The first Chapel on the left, dedicated to St. Sebastian, corresponds to the crypt below, from which the tombstone placed near the aisle has been brought.

The interior of the Basilica of San Sebastiano.

Above, The Catacombs of San Callisto.
The Crypt of St. Cecilia.

To the right, the Catacombs of San Callisto.
A hallway.

The Catacombs of St. Callisto

If the Catacombs of St. Sebastian are probably better known, due to their survival over the centuries, those of the Pope St. Callisto I (217-222) were of the greatest importance, as they served as the official cemetery of the original Christian community. The entrance opens near a small 3rd century Basilica which protects the tombs of Pope Zeffirino (217) and St. Tarcisio.

The cemetery is divided into several parts: the most important of them containing the remains of the popes, with the *Crypt of the Popes* at its centre. There are various 3rd century Martyr Popes buried here, in commemoration of whom Pope Damaso (366-384) ordered an epigraph be placed. He wanted to be buried near them, but as the epigraph declares, did not want to displace the bodies of his canonised predecessors. Next to it there is the *Crypt of St. Cecilia* where it is believed that Pope Pasquale I found the remains of the St., later transferred to the Basilica in Trastevere that bears her name. Besides the 7th to 8th century Byzantine style frescoes, the Crypt shows a reproduction of Stefano Maderno's famous 17th century statue representing St. Cecilia.

In a gallery near the Crypt of the Popes, there are the five cubicoli of the Sacraments (3rd century), named for the symbolic decorative themes. Of special interest is the cubicolum of the Five Saints, named for the painting with five blessed souls praying in Heaven, represented as a garden.

The original nucleus of the cemetery was probably the area of the *Crypts of Lucina*, in which we still admire important 2nd century frescoes, among the most ancient Christian pictorial art. They represent the Baptism of Christ, the Good Shepherd, souls in prayers, Daniel in the lions' den and symbolic figures, such as the eucharistic fishes.

The *Crypt of Pope Cornelius* (251-253) belongs to the same nucleus, and also features with pictorial decorations of following periods, representing various saints through the 6th century.

Many other galleries and crypts are worth visiting, although not all of them are accessible. It is enough to have seen a short, but meaningful example of this hidden world, in which the characteristics of the first centuries of Christianity are preserved with complete faithfulness.

The Catacombs of Domitilla

This is probably the widest underground cemetery complex of Rome, extending along Via Ardeatina (the entry faces Via delle Sette Chiese, No. 282). It was consecrated in the name of Domitilla, who is believed to have been Flavia Domitilla, wife of Flavio Clement; cousin of the Emperor Domitian, whose story is told by the Roman historian Suetonius: she was sentenced to death and her husband was exiled for their Christian faith. The noble woman gave the land, which at the beginning served even as a pagan burial ground (in fact, there are remains of cremation graves).

Starting the visit to the catacomb, we admire an unexpected view: a great underground basilica with three aisles, discovered only in 1874, after it was buried for almost a millennium. Scholars believe that it was buried because of an earthquake that probably took place in 897.

The Basilica had been consecrated in honour of the martyred Sts. Nereo and Achilleo (whose story is told in the beautiful epigraph of Pope Damaso), the first of the great, faithful Roman Martyrs. After its rediscovery it was restored, even though the damage caused by the earthquake left only of a part of the structure intact.

One of the most interesting parts of this complex is the so-called hypogeum of the Flavi, excavated under a small hill. The original entrance is beside the hill. It was attributed to the Imperial Family of the Flavi, to which Domitilla and her husband Flavio Clement belonged. In reality, the construction dates back to several different periods, but elements of considerable interest, such as the 3rd century paintings that decorate four niches in the large gallery, make this the most ancient portion of the so-called hypogeum. They represent, with singular elegance, cupids gathering grapes among vine leaves, vine branches and birds, and may be included among the first examples of known Christian painting. Of considerable interest it is the cubiculum called LOVE AND PSYCHE, which represents the famous pagan myth of Psyche who loses her groom after painful trials. The myth, symbolically interpreted, represents the immortality of the soul (Psyche) reached after having faced the trials of life. The style of the fresco, rather late, dates this decoration to the 3rd century AD.

After having become property of the Church, the cemetery was enormously enlarged with intersecting galleries which form the largest cemetery of Rome.

Its enlargement shows that it was used by quite a large Christian community. But when the tradition of Christians burial in underground galleries stopped in the 5th century, this cemetery was forgotten, except for the spots in which the bodies of the most venerated Martyrs had been buried, and the nearby underground Sanctuaries.

San Callisto. The Crypt of the Popes.

Below. The Catacombs of Domitilla. Inscriptions on a slab of marble with the symbols of the anchor and the fish.

Above. The Catacombs of Domitilla.
A hallway.

To the right, the Catacombs of San Callisto.
Inscriptions on a slab of marble.

Santa Croce in Gerusalemme

The memories of the Passion and the Death of Jesus, so full of light in the Scala Santa, have another residence a short distance from the Lateran complex: the Basilica of SANTA CROCE IN GERUSALEMME, also called "Sessoriana" or Eleniana.

It was built on behalf of the mother of Constantine before the pilgrimage to Jerusalem mentioned in the description of the Scala Santa. Nevertheless, after her return to Rome, the Holy Empress had a semi-underground chapel (actually consecrated to her) built, under which would be spread the soil from Calvary, which was brought from Jerusalem with other relics. This is the reason why the Basilica has the peculiar denomination of "in Jerusalem".

Very little remains of the original 4th century church, which has been restored many times over the centuries, the Basilica was almost entirely rebuilt in 1743 by Domenico Gregorini on behalf of Pope Benedict XIV. The *façade* is typical of the 18th century, with its quick and harmonious lines surmounted by statues of saints, while the Romanesque Bell Tower was built on behalf of Pope Lucius II in the middle of the 12th century.

The *interior* is divided into three naves, and features mostly 18th century decoration; only the Cosmatesque pavement recalls the earlier decor. On the ceiling, a fresco made by Corrado Giaquinto in 1714 represents the Ascent to Heaven of St. Helen. In the apse, we admire the 5th century fresco by Antoniazzo Romano, preserved from Gregorini's restoration, representing the "Rediscovery of the Cross".

The very precious fragments for which the Basilica is venerated, once kept in a valuable Reliquary, were moved to the modern CHAPEL OF THE RELICS on the upper floor, designed by the architect Florestano Di Fausto in 1930. The relics include three fragments of the Cross, a nail, a part of the title or "cartiglio" and two thorns of the crown imposed on Jesus for derision, while on the top of the staircase, behind a grating, is a transversal wing of the cross belonging to the "Buon Ladrone" (the "Good Thief").

While the parts of the Crosses, the nail and the thorn correspond to the Relics brought by St. Helen, we did not know anything about the "Title" until it was discovered by chance during some repair work in the Basilica in 1492, in a sealed drawer placed behind a mosaic.

The inscription, certainly tri-lingual, showed clearly the words J S NAZARENUS KING, and the legible corresponding words in Greek, while the ones with Hebrew types were not as readable.

This is a documentary element of great value; besides increasing the emotional aspect of the visit, it also assumes a historical meaning based on the millenary tradition of the "Basilica Eleniana".

The valuable work by Valadier with the reliquaries of Christ's Cross.

Santa Croce in Gerusalemme. The central nave.

San Lorenzo fuori le Mura

The patriarchal Basilica of San Lorenzo fuori le Mura (St. Lawrence Outside the Walls) is located next to Rome's monumental Verano cemetery. The original church, founded under Constantine in 330, and was later joined with another, wider church thought to have been built a century later under Sixtus III. The apses of both churches were demolished, and the primitive Basilica became the presbytery of the new great Basilica, to which the Romanesque bell tower was added in the 12th century. The *cloister*, another work of the Vassalletto family, was built in the 13th century.

During the 15th and 16th centuries, the Basilica suffered additional additions. Nevertheless, a restoration done under Pius IX between 1864 and 1870 relieved it of its baroque structures, returning the original purity of the church's lines. More substantial and difficult restoration were undertaken after a terrible air bombing that took place on July 19, 1943. Today, therefore, the Basilica of St. Lawrence is the result of this restoration that terminated in 1949.

The *façade* received character from the small but harmonious PORTICO with six Ionic columns made, as we have already mentioned, by the Vassalletto family, the famous marble makers. The back-wall of the portico is decorated with frescoes of the XIII century representing episodes of the life of Saint Lawrence and Saint Stephen; on the right, it is placed an imponent mass of marble on which there is an inscription in memory of the 1943 bombing that saw Pope Pius XII among the Romans hit by the disaster, with the white vest stained with the blood of the wounded. Opposite, the funeral *Monument in memory of Alcide De Gasperi*, the great Italian politician statesmen dead in 1954, extremely valuable work by Giacomo Manzù.

The ciborium.

On the right, the Basilica of San Lorenzo fuori le Mura

The interior of the Basilica of San Lorenzo.

The *Interior* is neat and severe, divided into three naves by twenty-two granite and cipolino columns taken from the ancient Roman monuments. The pavement, the two ambones, and the candlestick for the Easter candle are Cosmatesque masterpieces.

Next to the middle portal, on the right, there is the *Tomb of Cardinal Fieschi* (1256) with an ancient Roman sarcophagus placed under the canopy, restored after the serious damages suffered in the course of the unfortunate bombing. In the middle, on the High Altar, there is the valuable ciborium, made by a famous family of Roman marble workers, Paolo and sons, who signed and dated it in 1148. Under the High Altar there is the *Crypt of the Confession*, which protects the *relics of Sts. Lawrence, Stephen and Giustino.* The crypt partly reaches the elevated Presbytery, which corresponds to the Constantinian Basilica.

San Pietro in Vincoli

On a characteristic, isolated small square which is easily reached from the large road called Via Cavour, is another Basilica, ST. PETER IN CHAINS, which is object of a particular veneration for many reasons. It has very ancient origins, and is dedicated to a precious relic dating back to the earliest times of Christianity.

It was founded in the 5th century by the Empress Eudossia on the site of a pre-existing Basilica to hold the chains (vinculi in latin) of St. Peter, which had been discovered in Jerusalem.

The façade is of considerable interest. The elegant PORTICO, attributed to Baccio Pontelli or Meo del Caprino, was built for Cardinal Giuliano della Rovere, the future bellicose Julius II, who ordered Michelangelo to construct his own tomb. Most of the visitors go to the Basilica in order to admire the MOSES, a masterpiece which Michelangelo sculpted for the monument. The statue was to have been the main figure in a grandiose Mausoleum that was never built according to its original, majestic plan.

Although the monument is quite far from being the superb dream of the sculptor-architect, in which as many forty statues were to have been placed, the powerful figure of the biblical prophet is nevertheless among the most impressive figurative images in Western art. Moses is represented in an extremely simple position, still spreading a feeling of majesty beyond the words.

Omitting a minute illustration of the other, although extremely worthy, masterpieces contained in the Basilica, we make note of the golden bronze 19th century urn placed in the Confession, underneath the High Altar, which contains the Chains of St. Peter. The relics of the seven Maccabei Brothers, kept in the crypt in a Paleo-Christian burial sarcophagus decorated with episodes of the New Testament, is also an object of deep veneration.

The tomb of Pope Julius II by Michelangelo. At the center is the statue of Moses.

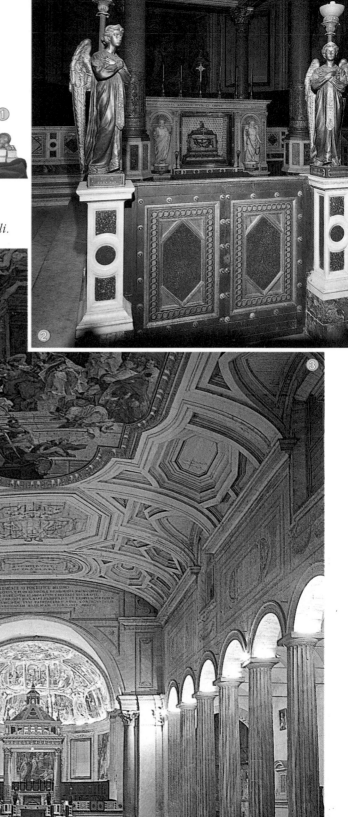

1 The chains that imprisoned St. Peter.
2 The Confession.
3 The interior of the Basilica of San Pietro in Vincoli.

Santa Maria in Aracoeli

Preeminently Roman for its history, its artwork and mostly for its marvellous and unique setting, *Santa Maria in Aracoeli* is one of the most venerated churches of the Eternal City. Founded in the 5th century, the church stands on the highest point of the Capitoline Hill. When Christian Rome displaced pagan Rome, the "Capitoline Basilica" took on a civil role in the new political-social context of the times, and served as the See of the Medieval Senate.

The Basilica is a stunning sight atop the long staircase of 124 steps, built in 1348 according to the wishes of the people which under the rule of Cola di Rienzo, after the terrible Black Death, which decimated the population of all Europe.

At the base of the steep stairway is a ramp that leads up to Michelangelo's beautiful Campidoglio, or Capitoline Square.

Not even the excessively white mass of the "Victorian", the colossal monument in memory of Vittorio Emanuele II, succeeds in taking

The façade of the Basilica, between the Campidoglio (on the right) and the Vittoriano (on the left).

The interior of the Basilica of Santa Maria in Aracoeli.

away the historical charm of the unpolished facade of the Basilica. Built in the 13th century, the Basilica is made with simple "brickwork", with three portals surmounted by as many round small windows, and a fourth rectangular window, which stands out in the middle.

Visitors normally enter the Basilica through the side entrance that leads to the right aisle. The *interior* has, according to the most classic tradition, three aisles subdivided into two lines of eleven columns (which are rather unequal, because they come from various Roman buildings); the pavement, according to the usual formula of the Roman Basilicas, is Cos-

matesque. The decorations of the wooden ceiling celebrate the victory of the Christian League against the Turks at Lepanto under Marcantonio Colonna, to whom the Senate conferred a "triumph" in the Basilica of Aracoeli, just like the leaders of the ancient Rome.

Next to the main entry we admire two important funeral monuments: the tombstone of the *Archdeacon of Aquileia, Giovanni Crivelli*, that bears the signature of Donatello, one of the founders of the Italian Renaissance art of Florence, and the *monument in memory of Cardinal d'Albert*, the work of Andrea Bregno, an important exponent of Lombard sculpture in the second half of the 15th century.

95

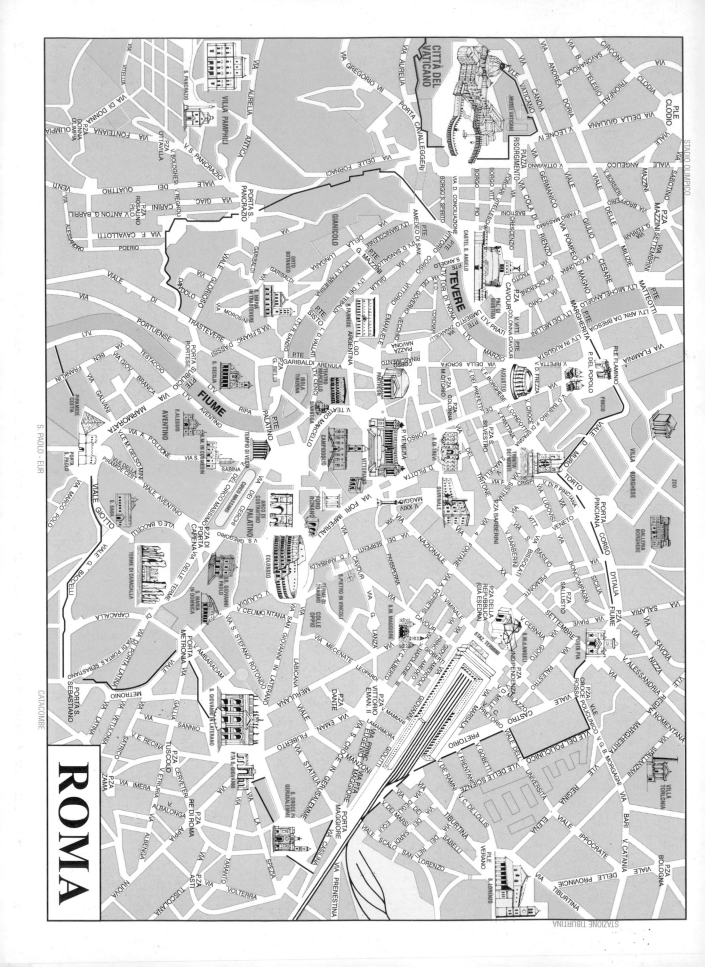

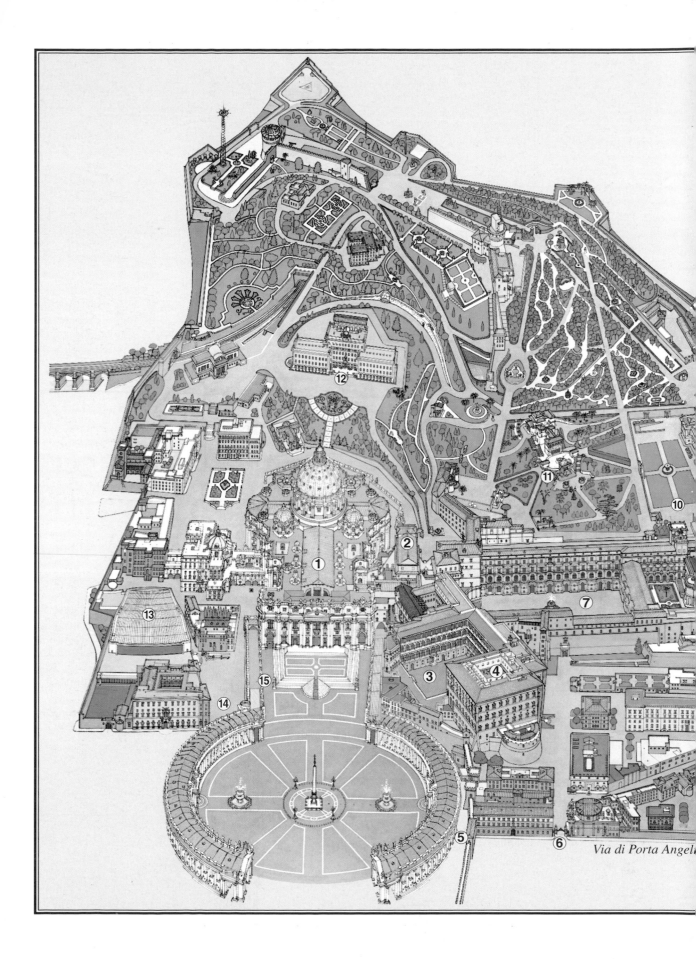

Via di Porta Angel

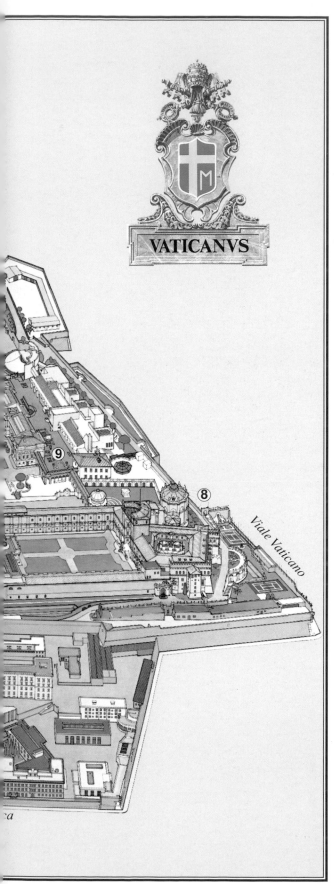

VATICANVS

PIANTA DEL VATICANO
MAP OF THE VATICAN - PLAN DU VATICAN
PLAN DES VATIKANS - PLANO DEL VATICANO - MAPA WATYKANU

① Basilica di San Pietro
(St. Peter's Basilica - Basilique de Saint-Pierre - Petersdom - Basílica de San Pedro - Bazylika św. Piotra)

② Cappella Sistina
(Sixtine Chapel - Chapelle Sixtine - Sixtinische Kapelle - Capilla Sixtina - Kaplica Sykstynska)

③ Cortile di San Damaso
(Court of St. Damasus - Cour de Saint-Damase - St. Damaso-Hof - Patio de San Damaso - Dziedziniec św. Damazego)

④ Palazzo Apostolico
(Apostolic Palace - Palais Apostolique - Die Päpstliche Wohnung - Palacio Apostólico - Pałac Apostolski)

⑤ Posta Vaticana e rivendita giornali
(Vatican Post Office and newsstand - Poste Vatican et Merchande de journaux - Vatikanpost und Zeitungsverkäufer - Correos y periodicos - Poczta Watykańska i kiosk)

⑥ Porta di Sant'Anna
(St. Anne Gate - Entrée de Sainte-Anne - Hl. Anne-Tor - Portal de Santa Ana - Brama św. Anny)

⑦ Cortile del Belvedere
(Court of "Belvedere" - Cour de Belvédère - Belvedere-Hof - Patio del Belvedere - Dziedziniec Belwederu)

⑧ Ingresso Musei Vaticani
(Entrance to the Vatican Museums - Entrée aux Musées Vaticanes - Eingang der Vatikanischen Museen - Entrada a los Museos Vaticanos - Wejście do Muzeów Watykańskich)

⑨ Pinacoteca
(Picture Gallery - Pinacothèque - Vatikanische Gemäldesammlung - Pinacoteca - Pinakoteka)

⑩ Cortile della Pigna
(Court of the "Pigna" - Cour del la "Pigna" - Pinienzapfenhof - Patio de la Piña - Dziedziniec "Pigna")

⑪ Casina di Pio IV
("Casino" of Pius IV - Maisonette de Pio IV - Haus Pius' IV - Palacete de Pío IV - Pałacyk Piusa IV)

⑫ Palazzo del Governatorato
(Palace of the Governorship - Palais du Gouvernatorat - Governatoratspalast - Palacio del Gobierno - Pałac Gubernatora)

⑬ Aula delle udienze pontificie Paolo VI
(Hall for the Papal Audiences "Paulus VI" - Salle des Audience Pontificales Paul VI - Päpstlicher Audienzsaal Paulus VI - Sala de las Audición Pontificias Pablo VI - Aula Pawłavi VI)

⑭ Ingresso all'Aula Paolo VI
(Entrance for Papal Audiences "Paulus VI" - Entrée à la Salle Paul VI - Audienzsaal. Eingang - Entrada al Aula Pablo VI - Wejściedo Auli im Pawła VI)

⑮ Ufficio informazioni turistiche del Vaticano
(Information bureau of the Vatican - Bureau de renseignements du Vatican - Auskunfstelle - Punto de información del Vaticano - Biuro informacji turystycznej w Watykanie).

BASILICHE PATRIARCALI

Patriarchal Basilicas - Basiliques Patriarcales -Patriarchal Basiliken
Basílicas patriarcales - Bazyliki Patriarchalne

SAN GIOVANNI IN LATERANO, Piazza San Giovanni in Laterano. ☎ 06 69886452.
SAN PAOLO FUORI LE MURA, Piazzale San Paolo. ☎ 06 5410178.
SAN PIETRO IN VATICANO, Piazza San Pietro. ☎ 06 69883462.
SANTA MARIA MAGGIORE, Piazza Santa Maria Maggiore. ☎ 06 483195.

BASILICHE

Basilicas - Basiliques - Basiliken - Basílicas - Bazyliki

SAN CLEMENTE, Piazza San Clemente. ☎ 06 70451018.
SAN LORENZO FUORI LE MURA, Piazzale del Verano, 3. ☎ 06 491511
SAN PIETRO IN VINCOLI, Piazza San Pietro in Vincoli, 4a. ☎ 06 4882865.
SAN SEBASTIANO FUORI LE MURA, Via Appia Antica, 136. ☎ 06 7808847
SANTA ANGNESE FUORI LE MURA, Via Nomentana, 349. ☎ 06 8610840
SANTA CECILIA IN TRASTEVERE, Piazza Santa Cecilia, 22. ☎ 06 5899289
SANTA CROCE IN GERUSALEMME, Piazza Santa Croce in Gerusalemme, 12. ☎ 06 7014769
SANTA MARIA IN ARACOELI, Piazza del Campidoglio, 4. ☎ 06 6798155.
SANTA MARIA IN TRASTEVERE, Piazza Santa Maria in Trastevere. ☎ 06 5814802.
SANTA MARIA DEGLI ANGELI, Piazza della Repubblica. ☎ 06 4880812.
SANTA PRASSEDE, Via Santa Prassede, 9a. ☎ 06 4882456
SANTA SABINA, Piazza Pietro d'Illiria, 1. ☎ 06 5743573
SANTI GIOVANNI E PAOLO AL CELIO, Piazza dei Santi Giovanni e Paolo, 13. ☎ 06 7005745

CHIESE E LUOGHI DI CULTO PRINCIPALI

Main Churches - Eglises - Kirchen - Iglesias - Kościoly

BATTISTERO LATERANENSE, Piazza San Giovanni in Laterano, 4. ☎ 06 69886452.
CHIESA DEL GESÙ, Via degli Astalli, 16. ☎ 06 6783602
CHIESA NUOVA (SANTA MARIA IN VALLICELLA), Piazza della Chiesa Nuova. ☎ 06 6875289
SAN GIORGIO IN VELABRO, Via del Velabro, 19. ☎ 06 6832930
SAN LUIGI DEI FRANCESI, Piazza San Luigi dei Francesi, 5. ☎ 06 688271
SAN MARCELLO AL CORSO, Piazza San Marcello, 5. ☎ 06 699301
SAN LORENZO IN LUCINA, Via in Lucina, 16a. ☎ 06 6871494
SAN PIETRO IN MONTORIO, Piazza San Pietro in Montorio, 2. ☎ 06 5813940
SANT'AGNESE IN AGONE, Piazza Navona. ☎ 06 6794435.
SANT'AGOSTINO IN CAMPO MARZIO, Via della Scofa, 80. ☎ 06 68801962
SANT'ANDREA DELLA VALLE, Piazza Vidoni, 6. ☎ 06 6861339
SANTA FRANCESCA ROMANA (S. MARIA NUOVA), Piazza S. Francesca Romana, 4. ☎ 06 6795528
SANTA MARIA DEL POPOLO, Piazza del Popolo, 12. ☎ 06 36.10.836.
SANTA MARIA IN COSMEDIN, Piazza Bocca della Verità, 18. ☎ 06 6781419
SANTA MARIA SOPRA MINERVA, Via Beato Angelico, 35. ☎ 06 6793926

SANTI AMBROGIO E CARLO AL CORSO, Via del Corso, 437. ☎ 06 6878335
SANTISSIMI COSMA E DAMIANO, Via dei Fori Imperiali, 1. ☎ 06 6991540
SANTISSIMA TRINITÀ DEI PELLEGRINI, Via dei Pettinari, 36a. ☎ 06 6868451
SANTUARIO DELLA MADONNA DEL DIVINO AMORE, Via Ardeatina Km 12. ☎ 06 71353302
SCALA SANTA, Piazza San Giovanni in Laterano. ☎ 06 70494489.
TRINITÀ DEI MONTI, Piazza Trinità dei Monti, 3. ☎ 06 6794179

CATACOMBE

Catacombs - Catacombes - Katakomben - Catacumbas - Katakumby

DOMITILLA, Via delle Sette Chiese, 280. ☎ 06 5110342.
PRISCILLA, Via Salaria, 430. ☎ 06 86206272
SANTA AGNESE, Via Nomentana,349. ☎ 06 8610840
SAN CALLISTO, Via Appia Antica, 110. ☎ 06 5136725.
SAN SEBASTIANO, Via Appia Antica, 136. ☎ 06 7887035.

INFORMAZIONI TURISTICHE

Tourist informaton - Auskünfte - Renseignements
Informaciones turisticas - Informacja turystyczna

AGENZIA ROMANA PER LA PREPARAZIONE DEL GIUBILEO - Viale G. Baccelli, 10 - ☎ 06 681671
APT (Rome Tourist Bureau) - Via Parigi, 5 - ☎ 06 488991
ENIT (National Tourist Bureau) - Via Marghera, 2 - ☎ 06 49711
Punti informativi del Comune di Roma (Rome Municipality Tourist Information Points):

Largo Goldoni - ☎ 06 68136061
Piazza San Giovanni in Laterano - ☎ 06 77203598
Lungotevere Castello - ☎ 06 68809707
Via dei Fori Imperiali - ☎ 06 69924307
Via del Corso, 189 - ☎ 06 69200435
Stazione Termini, Piazza dei Cinquecento.

NUMERI UTILI

Useful numbers - Numéros utiles - Nützlichetelefonnumern - Números útiles

AMBULANZE (Ambulances) . . . .☎ 06 55.10
CARABINIERI (Police) . . . . ☎ 112
POLIZIA STRADALE (Road police) . . . . ☎ 06 55.44
PRONTO SOCCORSO (Early Rescue) . . . . ☎ 118
SOCCORSO ACI (Road Assistance) . . . . ☎ 116
SOCCORSO PUBBLICO - POLIZIA (Police - First aid) . . . . . . ☎ 113
TAXI . . . . ☎ 06 3570 - 06 88177 - 06 4994 - 06 3875
VIGILI DEL FUOCO (Fire men) . . . . ☎ 115
VIGILI URBANI (City police) . . . . ☎ 06 67.691